the rules
of being a
Warner

first things first

{ Kurt & Brenda Warner }
with JENNIFER SCHUCHMANN

Tyndale House Publishers, Inc., Carol Stream, Illinois

Library of Congress Cataloging-in-Publication Data

Warner, Kurt, date.
    First things first : the rules of being a Warner / Kurt and Brenda Warner, with Jennifer Schuchmann.
        p. cm.
    Includes bibliographical references.
    ISBN 978-1-4143-3406-6 (hc)
        1. Family—Religious life. 2. Warner, Kurt, date. 3. Warner, Brenda. I. Warner, Brenda. II. Schuchmann, Jennifer, date. III. Title.
    BV4526.3.W37 2009
    280′.4092--dc22
    [B]   2009016790

Printed in the United States of America

15 14 13 12 11 10 09
 7   6   5   4   3   2   1

To our parents, who gave us passion,
our siblings, who gave us strength,
and our children, who give us purpose,
we dedicate this book to you.
Thank you for loving us.

CONTENTS

To many people, Kurt Warner is associated with his amazing quarterbacking abilities and his performances on the football field. He's known in the world of sports as an icon of excellence and talent. However, many more people, including me, know him and my mom, Brenda, in a totally different way. They are not only famous in the eyes of sports fans everywhere; they are also known for their incredible capacity to change lives. I don't know anything about football. I don't have to, though, to know that my parents are great.

This book has a lot to do with the other side of things: what goes on in their lives outside the realm of professional sports. There is a lot to be said about their charity work and their calling in life. But take it from me, their teenage daughter: There is a lot to be said about their normalcy as well. People in the spotlight often are unfairly credited with perfection when in reality, they're as normal as everyone else! Our living room is flooded with toys, and odds are, one of the twins didn't flush the toilet. I've wiped one little brother's vomit off another little brother; and my dad, as he will mention, is a pro at cleaning poop off any surface. We argue, we disagree, and we love each other, just like any other family. We're normal. That is something a lot of people have a hard time believing.

There are many areas in which my parents do not excel, including their rules about boyfriends and curfews, but no one asked me! They have, however, successfully ingrained in their children's hearts countless important lessons. I'm grateful to have been raised in a household where there is so much love. I don't always see eye to eye with my parents, but now that I'm getting ready to leave the nest and head to college, more is becoming clear about why they've done what they've done.

My parents have rules that were created to protect us, but they also have invested time in teaching us how to be independent, to love people actively, and to lead lives of excellence. My mom always emphasizes that we are self-sufficient, and she has, with a motherly sternness, taught us to stand on our own. I'm especially thankful for this now that I'm leaving, because I can take what she's taught me and confidently fend for myself at school in New York City. At the same time, my parents have exhibited what it means to love the people around us. We have had the amazing opportunity to spend our Christmases at orphanages and our Thanksgivings at local food shelters to serve God through serving his people. These opportunities have given us perspectives that we will carry for the rest of our lives and—I hope—elaborate on. My father has done an exceptional job of teaching his children to lead lives of honor and excellence, and he has done so mostly through example. He doesn't need to tell my brothers how to treat their wives when they grow up, because they've already seen firsthand how to do it with excellence.

What I would like readers to take away from this book is not the attitude that Kurt and Brenda Warner are perfect but that they are real, normal people who have experienced a lot and have a lot to say. They love God, each other, their kids, and the people God has sent them to reach. They stand for excellence and God's love, and they have amazing stories to tell.

—Jesse Warner

PROLOGUE

{ KURT'S INTRODUCTION }

I knew it was important to get it right the first time—there wouldn't be any second chances. I didn't have the control I would like to have had in this situation; there wasn't much time left, and I couldn't call an audible. I had to trust that those who had laid out the game plan knew what they were doing. We were all professionals, yet I was the one who had to make it happen.

It was a bright Sunday afternoon, and I stood in the middle of the green Astroturf. I hadn't properly warmed up. In fact, I hadn't expected anything to go like it had gone. I remember lots of shouting. I got the ball in my hands, but there was no chance to get rid of it. I dropped to my knees and then collapsed to the ground, vowing to hang on to the ball no matter how hard I was hit.

The biggest one got me first, his arm grinding into my back. I tried to support myself on my elbows as the bodies dove on top of me—a second, a third. My shoulders burned from the pain, and the blood rushed to my head.

People yelled from every direction. There was confusion and chaos. As I lifted my head, more bodies—a fourth, and then a fifth—piled on. Someone stepped on my calf. I wanted to scream, but I knew a camera was aimed at me, and I didn't want anyone to see my pain. I didn't say a word. My training had conditioned me to absorb the worst pain imaginable and never give my opponent the satisfaction of seeing me react.

From the corner of my eye, I saw two different-colored jerseys pile on. My shoulders gave a little from the weight. By my count, I now had seven bodies smothering my back.

Stay focused, stay focused. This must be what it feels like to be buried alive.

I struggled to keep the ball from squirting out from the pile. Someone's chin pounded my head, and I prayed that it would be over soon. I wasn't sure how much longer I could take it. I held my breath.

"Hold it . . . hold it . . . don't move!" the photographer shouted above the noise of the kids. "I got it! We're good to go."

As the kids climbed off me and the photographer concluded the photo session for the cover of this book, I thought about how badly I want you to know the *real* Kurt and Brenda Warner. I want you to see the off-the-wall things we say to each other and the way we parent our kids. Despite the craziness that goes on around us sometimes—like a photo shoot in our backyard—we're just real people.

The things we say often surprise people. For instance, we talk about sex. When I'm traveling, I'll say, "I can't wait to get home to be with my wife. It's been too long!" When people who know about my Christian faith hear me say things like that, it can shock them. "You can't talk about sex," they say. Or, even better, "You enjoy sex?" Sure I can, and yes, I do. I'm a married man who loves his wife, and sex is a very important part of our marriage.

But other things are important too. Like who gets up with the kids when we both want to sleep in, who pays the bills, and who cleans up when company comes over. We've created some rules in our family that we all try to live by, and so many people have asked about them that we thought a book would be the best way to share them.

I've asked Brenda to join me in writing this book. She has an amazing story of her own, and someday I hope she'll tell more of it than this book allows. But you need to know the basics of her story, because it's an important part of our story. I also want you to hear directly from her how we run our house, parent our kids, and love each other.

What you'll see is that we don't always agree—even on the rules we set for ourselves—but one thing we can agree on is that we love each other, we love our kids, and we love Jesus.

{ BRENDA'S INTRODUCTION }

I'm a storyteller. And as the wife of an NFL player and the mother of seven kids, I have lots of stories to tell. One day, I hope to tell them in my own book. But after the *New York Times* printed an article about the rules we use to train our kids, we had so many inquiries that we felt it was the right time to write a book that explained more about our marriage and our parenting philosophy—not because we have all the answers, but because so many people have been interested.

Like everybody else, we're just trying to figure it out as we go along, but some of what we said made people want to know more. So that's how this book started, as a way for us to share a few stories about what's worked for us.

For example, here's a story that illustrates how the football side of our lives and the day-to-day part come together. It was right after Kurt won his first Super Bowl, so it must have been sometime in 2000. He received an award for being "Man of the Year." All week long I asked him, "What have you done to be Man of the Year?" That was before we started our foundation or were active in the community, so I was like, "Seriously, Man of the Year? What makes *you* Man of the Year?"

"I won a Super Bowl?"

Kurt will tell you that even *he* couldn't come up with a good argument. But he wasn't going to turn it down. It became a joke for us.

So, we're getting ready to go to the event. Kurt threw on his tux, because that's all he had to do. I mean, he wakes up in the morning looking stunning. I was standing in the bathroom, trying to keep my belly roll inside my Spanx while putting on makeup, when I heard Kurt from down the hall.

"I smell poop."

Our son Kade was just a toddler at the time, and we both knew what had happened—he'd taken off his diaper.

I heard Kurt looking for him. "Kade. Kade! Where are you?" Then I heard, "Oh, no! You won't believe what Kade's done."

"What?" I yelled as I squeezed into my evening gown.

"He's finger painted all over the glass door. With poop."

So I yelled back, "What makes you Man of the Year?"
And he said, "I'll get it."

That's the kind of stuff that goes on all the time in our house. We know we're at home cleaning poop off the glass, but all the public sees is "Man of the Year."

We have a great marriage, but it's not perfect. We still argue. Last week we had a huge blowup over jealousy. We're eleven years into our marriage, and sixteen years together, and these things still happen. But we're still together.

There have been ups and downs—good times and bad times in the Warner house over the past few years—and we think we've learned a few things through that process. That's what this book is about. We don't have ten steps to a perfect marriage or six easy ways to parent a teen, but we do have a few rules in our relationship that have worked for our family. Maybe a version of the rules can work for yours.

We don't want to come across like we have it all together, because we're still learning. We have our shortcomings and make mistakes just like everyone else. But we have so much fun. We find a lot of humor in each other and in our kids. There are belly laughs in our house every day. And most of all, we really appreciate what we have and what we've been given.

That's because we didn't always have it.

As you read this book, you'll see that Kurt starts each chapter from his perspective, and then I give mine. This is intentional. In our marriage, even though Kurt is more famous and makes more money, or whatever, we have equal voices, and we both shape our relationship and our parenting.

The first part of the book summarizes our story. Our past holds an important influence over who we are and how we parent. A lot's been said about our lives, and a lot of it has been wrong. We don't intend for this to be an autobiography; Kurt has already written his, and like I said, I'd still like to write mine someday. But we know that some people haven't heard our story and that there is a lot of misinformation out there, so in the first part of the book we just want to set the record straight.

Starting in chapter 4, we'll share the rules we've come up with to hold everything together. You'll join us for a day in the life of the Warners. With seven kids, our house is never boring. And when you take kids on the road, well, crazy things can happen—like the time Zack told Fergie of the Black Eyed Peas, "You stink. You stink." We'll also talk about our marriage and our relationship—the good, the bad, the belly rolls, and the belly laughs. We hope you'll find a few rules that will work for your own family and marriage.

In the last chapter, we summarize with some parting thoughts on what the rules really mean to us. We don't have all the answers, but we've found some things that work. We hope you will too.

CHAPTER 1

football Warner style

{ KURT }

Stupid! You're so stupid! You just lost your team the Super Bowl!

With less than eighteen seconds remaining in the second quarter, I'd just thrown the pass that I thought would give us the lead in Super Bowl XLIII. But as soon as the ball left my hand, my stomach hit the ground. Defensive Player of the Year James Harrison emerged from behind the helmets. I watched in horror as the ball hit him right between the numbers.

Screened by a blitzing player and my offensive linemen, I hadn't seen Harrison in the passing lane. What I thought would be a Cardinals touchdown turned into a mad scramble to stop Harrison from scoring at the other end of the field. I did my best to slow him down enough for one of my team-mates to tackle him, but as I lay on the turf watching him weave down the field, all I could think of was how stupid I was. Harrison scored the touchdown that gave the Steelers a ten-point halftime lead.

Even at moments like that, I love my job. When I'm
on the field, my mind is totally focused there. I don't
scan the stands looking for celebrities in attendance. I don't
notice the jeers being hurled at me from opposing fans.
I don't smile at my kids or wave to my wife during the game.
When I'm on the field, I'm locked in. Even after a play like
the interception by James Harrison, I was laser focused on
finding an opportunity to make up for my mistake.

In the fourth quarter, I got that opportunity. Down 20–7,
we knew if we wanted to make a comeback, we would have to
open up our offense and throw the ball. For as long as I can
remember, those are the times when I've been the most comfortable on the football field—with the ball in my hands, taking charge and dictating the tempo of the game.

Our offense had started clicking in the second half. We
had scored once and had gotten a safety, forcing the Steelers
up against the ropes. With three minutes remaining in the
game, we were down by just four points. We had the ball and
the momentum. Now was our chance.

We stayed in the spread offense. My plan was to get the
ball to Larry Fitzgerald or Anquan Boldin, placing our fate
in the hands of two of our best players and allowing them
to make plays. The Steelers knew they were having trouble
stopping us and had chosen to play a two-man coverage. So,
against the league's best defense and one of the most difficult
coverages to throw against, I called my favorite play to attack
them.

As I took the snap and scanned the field, I knew the odds
were good that Larry or Anquan would be open. My first read

on the play was to Larry, and I saw that he had gotten a great jump at the snap and had separated from his defender. He caught the ball in the open field and ran sixty-four yards into the end zone.

With 2:37 left to go in the Super Bowl, we had just taken the lead. It was the first time I allowed myself to think, *We just might be the World Champions!*

Of course, we all know what happened. The Steelers came back with less than a minute on the clock, preventing us from achieving the first Cardinals championship in franchise history.

After eleven years in the NFL, I think I finally have the proper perspective on winning and losing. Losing still stinks. But what happens on the field—whether it's the highest of highs or the lowest of lows—doesn't define me as a person.

Most people think that the stories I'll tell after a Super Bowl will be like the one above—a game-changing moment of threading a great pass through a field of defensive players to the waiting hands of my receiver. Others have seen enough media coverage about me to assume I'll tell stories about how I prayed to Jesus for our team to win. Nothing could be further from the truth. The stories I tell the most are not necessarily exciting to reporters, but I think they're more important.

After my Super Bowl win with the Rams in 1999, my favorite story to tell was one about my kids. I had three kids at the time, and none of them came to the big game. They thought football was "boring."

When the game was over, I couldn't wait to call them.

I was in the locker room with my agent, Rob Lefko, who wanted to prep me for a press conference the next day. I had been named Most Valuable Player, and there would be a lot of media attention. I asked him to wait a minute while I called home to talk to my kids.

The phone rang a couple of times before Zack, my oldest, who was nine at the time, answered the phone. Here's what the conversation sounded like from Rob's perspective:

"Hey, buddy! Daddy just won the Super Bowl. . . . Uh huh . . . Did you watch any of the game? . . . Uh huh . . . Okay . . ." And then before I could say, "I love you . . . ," he was gone.

I turned to Rob and said, "Zack wasn't interested. He was watching Veggie Tales."

The point of the story isn't that my kids do funny stuff; it's that my children remind me that football isn't the most important thing in our world. And I love that! I love that my kids aren't preoccupied with my football career. Ten years later, three kids has turned into seven, but not much has changed about their attitude toward football.

Zack's now nineteen. He is in his fifth year of high school, and he is learning how to live independently. He's legally blind, but after watching him get around, you would never know it. Brenda will tell you more about Zack when she tells you her story.

Jesse is seventeen. I met her when she was nine months old, and we didn't exactly hit it off. But now she's heading off to college and I can't imagine life without her.

Kade is ten. He's our big boy. He plays Pop Warner

football, but he doesn't like it much. Brenda once caught me in the backyard trying to pay him a quarter for each pass he caught, but she put a stop to that.

Jada just turned eight. She's our little fashionista, and she's a vegetarian. I'm not sure if she's a vegetarian because she cares so much about animals or because she doesn't like her mother's cooking.

Elijah is five. He's the only one who really cares about football. And he always knows the scores. When I come in after a game, he's always quick to remind me, "Dad, you lost!" Nice, huh?

Sienna and Sierra are our three-year-old twins, affectionately called "Babygirls." Sienna is bigger than Sierra and can often be found hiding out in the snack pantry. Sierra is smaller but spunky like her mother. We often describe their personalities as sweet and spicy.

This year, the oldest five kids got to choose whether or not they wanted to attend the Super Bowl. We didn't give the Babygirls a choice. Zack chose not to come; his hearing has developed to compensate for his blindness, so he finds the fireworks at football games uncomfortably loud. Jesse wanted to come. Brenda wonders if the only reason was because she wanted to be on TV. I'd like to think it was to support her dad, but either way, I was fine with it. Kade, like I said, is playing Pop Warner football, so he's just starting to get into it a bit. He decided he wanted to come. Elijah does whatever Kade does, so of course he was in. That left Jada. At first she wanted to come because everyone else was going. Then she didn't want to waste a whole day watching football.

Sometimes when Brenda takes the kids to my games, they just fall asleep—which is good, because at least they're not bothering her while she's trying to watch the game. But this time, Brenda thought the kids should be there for the memories. She kept saying, "What if this is your last Super Bowl?" But I didn't want the kids to come to the game just because Dad was in the Super Bowl. I don't care if five years from now I have a picture of them in my arms with confetti falling around us. I don't even care if they remember I played football.

In the end, Jada decided to stay home.

Three days after the game, Jada seemed upset. "What's wrong, beautiful?" I asked.

"Dad," she said, "I *really* wanted to go to the Super Bowl."

That surprised me, because just days earlier she had said that going to the Super Bowl would be a waste of time. Had I missed something?

Brenda explained it to me later. "When Jada went back to school, all her friends mentioned how they saw her brothers and sister on TV, so now Jada wishes she had gone just so her friends would have seen *her* on TV too."

But here's the funny part: When the cameras showed my family, no one saw Kade because he was tucked inside his hoodie playing with his Nintendo DS rather than watching the game. Some of our friends watching the game on TV didn't even know that Kade had gone with us.

So that's football at the Warner house. Girls who want

to get on TV and boys who want to be left alone to play their DS.

{ BRENDA }

At the Super Bowl we were all sitting in the same row. It was me, then Jesse, then Elijah, then Kade. The game was in the third quarter. *The third quarter.* You know, the one after the huge halftime extravaganza?

I heard Elijah say, "Momma, Momma."

He said it over and over and over, and finally I'm like, "*What*, Elijah?"

"Is this the Super Bowl or just a normal game?"

"It's the Super Bowl, Elijah. This is the third quarter."

I focused back on the game, but a couple minutes later I heard Elijah again.

"Jesse. Jesse. Jesse. What's an armadillo?"

"Mom, Elijah wants to know what an armadillo is."

Did I mention that it was the third quarter—*of the Super Bowl*? And all I'm getting is, "What's an armadillo?"

Prior to the game, all they could talk about was getting a puppy. They'd seen the news coverage when Barack Obama had promised his girls a puppy if he won the election. Our kids also wanted a dog, and they tried to talk Kurt into getting one. Kurt, of course, didn't want anything to do with it. So about halfway through the season, I said, innocently enough, "Well, how about Dad gets you a puppy if he wins the Super Bowl?" And the kids all started yelling, "Yeah, Daddy! Yeah, Daddy!" The little ones really know how to work it.

So Kurt said, "I could *probably* agree to that, because we're not going to the Super Bowl." That's exactly what he said—the emphasis was on the *probably*.

But somehow it became a pact. When the kids brought up the puppy topic, Kurt would say, "*If* we go . . . ," and the kids would say, "*When* you go . . . ," But Kurt wasn't worried, because at that point in the season, no one, including Kurt, thought the Cardinals would be in the Super Bowl.

Then the playoffs started.

The way I remember it happening is that a reporter asked Kurt, "Are your kids excited about the playoffs?"

He said, "No, not really. All they care about is that Mom promised them a puppy if we win the Super Bowl."

When I read that, I couldn't believe that Kurt had told the media. Then it became a big deal. At every game, people would ask Kurt, "You get a puppy yet?" or "Did you pick out your puppy?" We started getting leashes and dog dishes in the mail.

So when the Cardinals actually made it to the Super Bowl, the children's thoughts apparently had little to do with football and everything to do with animals—puppies and armadillos.

When the game ended, Kade started crying when he realized we had lost. Bawling. He's a gentle giant, and I assumed his heart was broken for Daddy.

Then Kurt ran over to our front-row seats. I didn't think he would. Usually, he only does that when he wins. He told me later that he knew the kids would be upset, and he wanted them to know he was okay.

So, as he was standing on the field, he said to Kade, "Hey, buddy."

Kade was still crying big crocodile tears.

Kurt said, "It's okay; it's going to be okay. It's just a game. I love you all, and I'll talk to you in a little while."

As we left the stadium, it was total chaos. We had to walk through a bunch of Steelers fans, and, of course, we were wearing red. People yelled stuff—"Go, Steelers!"—right into the kids' faces. When we finally got to our car, Kade had again pulled his hood over his head so no one could tell he was crying.

As we got into the car, Elijah started bawling too. Now, I know he doesn't understand the game, so I didn't know what he was crying about. But he kept crying and crying, until finally he calmed down just enough for me to talk to him.

"Elijah, what are you still crying about?"

He sniffled, his lip quivered, and then he finally got it out: "We're not getting a puppy. Daddy lost the Super Bowl!"

We laughed about it, but Elijah continued to cry.

I'm writing this a month after the Super Bowl. We still haven't gotten a puppy.

Kurt is holding out.

CHAPTER 2

red boots and pink bathrobes

{ KURT }

So much has been written about Brenda and me in the media that people think they know us. But most people don't know the real story. Sure, the media portray parts of our lives, but they're just as likely to get it wrong as they are to get it right.

For example, have you seen this widely circulated e-mail?

KURTIS THE STOCK BOY AND BRENDA THE CHECKOUT GIRL

This is a true story.

In a supermarket, Kurtis the stock boy was busily working when a new voice came over the loudspeaker asking for a carryout at register 4. Kurtis was almost finished, wanted to get some fresh air, and decided to answer the call. As he approached the checkout stand, a distant smile caught his eye. The new checkout girl was beautiful. She was an older woman (maybe 26; he was only 22), and he fell in love.

Later that day, after his shift was over, he waited

by the punch clock to find out her name. She came into the break room, smiled softly at him, took her card and punched out, then left. He looked at her card: BRENDA. He walked out only to see her start walking up the road. Next day, he waited outside as she left the supermarket and offered her a ride home. He looked harmless enough, and she accepted. When he dropped her off, he asked if maybe he could see her again, outside of work. She simply said it wasn't possible.

He pressed, and she explained she had two children and she couldn't afford a babysitter, so he offered to pay for the babysitter. Reluctantly, she accepted his offer for a date for the following Saturday. That Saturday night, he arrived at her door only to have her tell him that she was unable to go with him. The babysitter had called and canceled. To which Kurtis simply said, "Well, let's take the kids with us."

She tried to explain that taking the children was not an option, but again not taking no for an answer, he pressed. Finally Brenda brought him inside to meet her children. She had an older daughter, who was just as cute as a bug, Kurtis thought. Then Brenda brought out her son, in a wheelchair. He was born a paraplegic with Down syndrome.

Kurtis asked Brenda, "I still don't understand why the kids can't come with us." Brenda was amazed. Most men would run away from a woman with two kids, especially if one had disabilities—just like her first husband and father of her children had done. Kurtis was not ordinary—he had a different mind-set.

That evening, Kurtis and Brenda loaded up the kids, went to dinner and the movies. When her son needed anything, Kurtis would take care of him. When he needed to use the restroom, he picked him up out of his wheelchair, took him, and brought him back. The kids loved Kurtis. At the end of the evening, Brenda knew this was the man she was going to marry and spend the rest of her life with.

A year later, they were married, and Kurtis adopted both of her children. Since then they have added two more kids.

So what happened to Kurtis the stock boy and Brenda the checkout girl? Well, Mr. and Mrs. Kurt Warner now live in Arizona. If you tune in on 1 February, you can watch him quarterback the Arizona Cardinals in the Super Bowl against the Pittsburgh Steelers![1]

Inspiring story.

But it's not true.

Most people find the real story even more inspiring than the e-mail version. That's why I want you to know the truth about how Brenda and I really got together.

It was 1992, my fourth year of college and my third year of football eligibility at the University of Northern Iowa. Football wasn't going very well. I wasn't the starting

quarterback, and it looked as if I wouldn't get that opportunity until my final year of eligibility. I had just turned
twenty-one, and some friends talked me into hanging out
at a bar called Wild E. Coyotes. I wasn't much of a drinker
(though there were some exceptions to that rule), and I didn't
like country music. But the crowd was different from what I
found on campus, and perhaps more important, my friends at
the bar never asked why I wasn't starting. The country music
grew on me. The bar was a great place to meet friends, hang
out, and dance (though I wasn't a very good dancer). Before I
knew it, I was a regular.

I remember a girl who stood out from the crowd. She had
her own look—short dark hair and an air of confidence in the
way she carried herself. She wore cowgirl stuff. Denim mini-
skirts and red boots. She was different from the other girls—
certainly from the college girls I was used to dating. I'd watch
her on the dance floor sometimes; she was good, better than
I was anyway. Whatever it was, she intrigued me, but never
enough for me to leave my friends and go talk to her.

I had a lot of friends at the bar. If you ask Brenda now,
she'd say that when I came in the door, people would make
their way over to me like fish going upstream. She remembers
I had feathered hair and an attitude. Her mom pointed me
out to her once, and they both laughed and made comments
like, "He thinks he's all that." I obviously don't remember
that.

I do remember having lots of friends. And, of course,
because I was a football player, I met lots of girls at those
Wild E. Coyote nights; but I was never all that interested

in any of them. I wasn't the kind of guy who was looking for a quick hook-up; I had goals and things I wanted to accomplish in life. Most of the college girls I knew didn't have goals. So, for me, those nights at the bar weren't about picking up a girl; they were about celebrating football victories or escaping from the campus scene for a while. But while I was there, I had a good time.

One night, while doing the Barn Dance, a line dance where you change partners every sixteen counts, I found myself standing in front of that intriguing girl in the red boots. Two steps to the right, two steps to the left; I twirled her, then twirled her back, we bowed, and the song ended.

"Do you want to keep dancing?" I asked her.

"I'd love to," she said.

"What's your name?"

"I'm Brenda."

"Glad to meet you, Brenda. I'm Kurt."

At the end of each song, I asked her if she'd like to keep dancing, and she said yes. After a few songs, I stopped asking; we just kept dancing. Slow song, fast song, no matter what it was, we stayed on the floor. Before I knew it, it was 1:30, and someone yelled, "Last call!"

At 2:00 they played the last song and blinked the lights, telling us it was time to leave.

I walked with Brenda to her friend's car. I think I was hoping to get her phone number, but before I could ask, she turned to me and said, "Before you leave, I want you to know something. I'm divorced, and I have two kids."

"Really?"

"Yeah. So if you never want to see me again, I understand."

I was shocked. I remember thinking, *You've been married* and *divorced?* It's not what I expected. I mean, I knew there was something different about her; she seemed more mature. But never in a million years would I have guessed she was divorced and the mother of two. In college you don't meet people like that—at least not people you're attracted to.

My first thought was, *This isn't going to work.* But then I thought, *Why not? What's the real hang-up?*

Still wrestling with what she'd just told me, I leaned over and kissed her on the cheek.

"Good night."

"Good night."

After she left, I kept replaying the conversation in my mind, *"I'm divorced, and I have two kids. If you never want to see me again, I understand."*

Her words grabbed me. In the past, I'd been serious with girls, but what was serious about it? I mean, it was still lame and still superficial. There wasn't a whole lot of depth to the relationship; it wasn't about life moving forward. It was just about the now.

Maybe that's what intrigued me about Brenda. Her words were a reminder that I needed to start thinking about life, not just wait for college to end and then say, "Now what?"

I think that's what drew me in. It was a challenge, a different view on things. Maybe it was something more substantial.

In any case, I didn't want her walking away saying, *"Oh, there he goes, another guy who runs away because of two kids."* Even if we didn't end up dating, I wanted her to know it had

nothing to do with her situation. We could still be friends.
I liked her. And like I said, there was something different
about her.

So maybe it was the intrigue or just the curiosity, but I
thought, *Let's meet her kids. Let's see what they're like.*

{ BRENDA }

There was a knock on the sliding glass door.

Without thinking, I opened the blinds and saw Kurt—
I didn't even know his last name—standing on the step, holding a single rose. Two thoughts ran through my mind almost
simultaneously: *Cute guy from the bar. This is the last thing
I need* and, because I was still breastfeeding Jesse, *I hope my
breasts aren't leaking milk right now.*

This was the first time I'd seen Kurt without a crowd following him. There was something special about him, almost a light
around him. And he was a good dancer. But until we'd danced
the night before, I'd never even bothered to speak to him.

It had been my mom's idea that I get out more, and she
was the one who urged me to go to Wild E. Coyote's. I'd
been divorced about seven months. Zack was three years old,
and Jesse was nine months. I lived in my parents' house, sold
Mary Kay cosmetics during the day, took prerequisite classes
for nursing school at night, and survived on food stamps.
When some women from my mom's church decided to take
line-dancing lessons, Mom dragged me along with them. She
thought it would be good for me to get out and meet people.

Most of my high school friends had moved on to college
or jobs, so I didn't have a lot of friends at that time. Mom and

I took lessons while Dad watched the kids. Then Mom would go home to be with Dad, and she'd encourage me to stay at the bar and practice what we learned. I wasn't a big drinker, but I liked to dance. So after the lessons, I'd hang out, meet some friends, and dance. My rule was that I'd dance with anyone who had enough nerve to ask me. But after all I'd been through, the last thing I was trying to do was pick up a guy in a bar. Even if he was cute.

The Internet story got a couple of things right. I was the divorced mother of two. And Jesse *was* cute as a bug. But she wasn't the oldest. That honor belongs to Zack, who was neither a paraplegic nor born with Down syndrome. But I'm getting ahead of myself.

While still in high school, I decided to join the Marine Corps. My sister, "the smart one," was already in college, and family finances were tight. Because I was "the pretty one," college wasn't considered an option; after graduation, I headed straight to boot camp.

I loved it. The Marines fit my personality, and I did well. I got a lot of attention and was promoted quickly.

While at Marine Intelligence School in Florida, I met Neil. He was the best in his platoon. He scored higher than anyone else on physical-fitness tests; had an incredible, muscular build; and looked handsome in his uniform. Everyone looked up to him, and yet for some reason, he noticed me. I fell in love with him, and we started dating.

Then we got orders. His were to Cuba, and mine were to Okinawa. It didn't take long before he wrote me a letter saying there was no way it would work. So we broke up. It was hard at first, but I got over it. I started dating other Marines, enjoying life, and learning to scuba dive. Eventually, I got orders for New Orleans.

While I was in New Orleans, Neil called. He'd been discharged from the Marines and said he wanted to come visit me. I began to think, *It's fate* or, perhaps more in line with my beliefs, *It's God bringing us back together!*

When I saw Neil again, he explained that he'd had a medical discharge due to a brain tumor that caused seizures. The medication wasn't controlling the seizures, and he couldn't drive for at least six months. There was no way he could keep a job. I should have run at that point, but what I thought was, *Okay, now I have to take care of him.* So he moved in, and I continued to work.

My parents weren't happy with the living-together situation. In fact, they were embarrassed. No one in my world did that, and here I was supposed to be a "good Christian woman." So on St. Patrick's Day 1988, Neil and I went to city hall, plunked down $50, and got married by a justice of the peace. Nothing romantic about it.

Three months later, not only had I reenlisted, but I had orders to move to Virginia Beach, Virginia. And then I got pregnant. We planned for Neil to be a stay-at-home dad because I was the one bringing in the income. I had an easy pregnancy, and Zack was born healthy and happy. After four weeks of maternity leave, I went back to work.

On September 6, when Zack was about four months old, I was at work when I got a call from Neil.

"Zack's not breathing right."

"What do you mean, Zack's not breathing right?" I asked.

"I don't know. He's just not breathing right. Why don't you come home?"

The ER was so close that we drove Zack there ourselves. After a quick examination, they immediately put Zack in an ambulance and took him to the big naval hospital. I was twenty-one years old and following an ambulance with my infant son in it. My hands trembled as I tried to drive. We didn't have any idea what was going on.

The next few hours were a blur. They kept asking us what happened, and we didn't have any answers.

"I was giving him a bath and everything was going well. Then he stopped breathing," Neil told them over and over again.

They did a spinal tap to check for meningitis, but the results came back negative. His brain started swelling, yet the doctors were still searching for a cause. This contin-ued through the night. When I was finally allowed into his room, I saw that he was having seizures. Zack's head was huge because the soft spots in his skull had expanded from the pressure of fluid that was building up. The fluid filled the soft areas and throbbed. Zack cried like crazy, and the doctors told me things that didn't make sense.

"His retinas have hemorrhaged. He will be completely blind."

Looking out the window at the traffic zooming by where two highways joined together, I wanted to scream, "Stop! Everybody just stop!" The world was moving so fast, and my son was dying. Instead, I silently prayed, *God, you've got to step in here. He's dying.*

The doctors said, "His brain is still swelling. We're going to have to pop open the soft spot and let the fluid release." Zack was in so much pain. They took that itty-bitty chubby little body with dimples, four months old, completely blind now, and they drained the soft spot.

A couple of hours later, they had to drain it again. And again.

Twenty-four hours later, we still didn't know what was going on. Neil's parents lived near us, and they had come to the hospital. They drank coffee with him downstairs while I sat alone in a cold white room just praying that my baby would live.

Finally, my father-in-law came in and said, "Neil needs to tell you something, and you just need to let him say what he needs to say. Then we're going to deal with this."

He left, and Neil walked in. I could tell he'd been crying. He sat down next to me and started weeping. "I dropped him," he said.

"What do you mean, you dropped him?"

"I was giving him a bath, and I accidentally dropped him." His words were almost unintelligible as he cried uncontrollably, "I am so sorry."

I remember reassuring him, "It was an accident; you didn't mean to."

Neil's dad had left to tell the doctors what happened. Neil and I hadn't even finished talking before a crowd of doctors and nurses packed into the small room and started asking lots of questions. Child Protective Services was called. Over the next few days, as the doctors put together a treatment plan to keep Zack alive, Neil and I were interrogated by social workers. Everything became an accusation.

"Why didn't you tell anyone right away?"

Neil was too scared to say much. "It was an accident," I'd tell them. "Neil accidentally dropped him."

"What's the bruise on his arm?"

I'm thinking, *What bruise?*

They separated us to ask more questions and sent people to watch us interact with Zack. Charges were investigated, and we weren't allowed to see Zack without a monitor. Though I now understand what they were doing, at the time, I couldn't figure out why they just didn't believe it was an accident.

Zack kept having seizures. He was in a horrible metal bed that looked like a cage. Sitting in the chair next to his bed, I could see his tiny pinkie finger twitch, and I would get up and go to him. The seizures started with a tremor in his right pinkie, and then they'd spread to his face, and he'd start to shake. Full-out grand mal seizures. I knew what they were because I had watched Neil have them.

Scared for Zack's life, I'd cry and claim promises from Scripture. Verses I had read in the Bible as a teenager were thrown back at God as I begged him to heal Zack's body.

I wish I could say that Zack was cured, completely healed. But six weeks later—after a CPS hearing at which there wasn't enough evidence to prove child abuse—he was still in the hospital.

A few days after the hearing, my mom and I were back in his hospital room wondering what would come next. I could tell the doctors were surprised that Zack was still alive, but there wasn't anything else they could do for him. It was so sad.

They'd check his vital signs, but I think they kept him there just because I was a young mother and they didn't know what else to do with him.

So there I was, twenty-one years old, with a husband on the couch at home still trying to regulate his own seizure medication, and now a baby in the hospital who would be on the same medication for the rest of his life.

That's when I formed a plan. If I'd had my way, I would have been a lifer in the Marines. Instead, I asked for and received a hardship discharge. Then I asked the doctor if we could take Zack back to Iowa. With my mom there, it made it easier to convince him. I remember the doctor saying, "You'll be lucky if he ever sits up."

"So that's as good as it's going to get?" I asked.

He said, "You'll be *lucky* if he ever sits up. Hear me right: *lucky*."

And I remember my mom just rubbing my back.

Neil and I moved back to Cedar Falls with my parents. Neil got his seizures under control, applied for work at the post office, and got a job in Cedar Rapids. We moved into a tiny two-bedroom house bought on a VA loan for $52,000. It was located on K Avenue near Regis High School.

To get outside and get some exercise, I would walk Zack in a stroller around the high school track. Sometimes, the football team would be practicing, and I would think, *Could you guys please be quiet?* They were so loud, and I wanted Zack to rest. Little did I know at the time that *that* was Kurt's high school team practicing.

My days were spent taking care of Zack. I'd take him to neurologists, pediatric ophthalmologists, and regular doctor appointments. I had a full-time job making sure he got what he needed. He had physical therapy, occupational therapy, and therapy at home that I took care of. I hated stretching his muscles and making him cry, or patching his good eye so his weak one would get stronger, but I knew it would all benefit him. Mostly, I just wanted to hold him and love him. I did that, too.

On Sunday, I'd go to church alone, because Neil worked nights and slept during the day. I'd think, *God, I need you. I need your strength.* Even when I didn't see results from my prayers, I'd tell God, "I'm not giving up. I am not backing down. I don't understand it, but I know you love me and you love Zack." I also cried a lot during that time.

Eventually, my work paid off, and we began to see progress.

During that time, Neil was still filled with guilt, and it wore me out trying to help him deal with it. God may not have healed Zack completely, but every time I looked at him, I saw his continued life as a miracle from God. Neil didn't see it that way. Every time he looked at his son, it was a reminder of all that Zack couldn't do or would never be. Zack was blind guilt staring Neil in the face.

Nevertheless, things were going well in Cedar Rapids. We could pay our bills week by week, and we had great insurance coverage because of Neil's job at the post office. We had a normal life—or at least things were flowing. So Neil and I decided to have another baby. I hoped it would bring us closer together. I'd seen how babies could bring such joy to a family, and I felt that we could use some joy.

Life wasn't what I'd planned. I'd given up my career and my identity. I had a child with special needs. I had a husband who had regained control of his medical issues to become stable and productive but was now dealing with the emotional consequences of his past. It wasn't Disney World, but whose marriage is? I was a Marine, and I was capable of making anything work.

"Why are you so distant?" I'd ask Neil.

"I'm not. You're just hysterical. Your hormones are wacky because you're pregnant."

We'd fight. We'd fight a lot. So what? My parents fought over money for years, and they loved each other. I didn't believe in walking out. This was the marriage I'd been given, and I'd do whatever it took to make it work.

When I was eight months pregnant, Neil and I were on an hour-long drive home from my grandfather's funeral. I remember our conversation—what little there was.

"Is there something going on? You seem so distant," I asked.

"Nope. I'm fine."

"You sure? You don't seem like it. Do you still . . . do you still love me?" I remember asking him that.

And I remember his answer. "Um, yep, I still love you." I could read his answer like a temperature gauge in an Iowa winter—cold.

When we got home and got into bed, I started thinking about how long it had been since he'd touched me. *Is it the pregnancy?*

"You haven't touched me in a long time. Do you still find me attractive?"

"Yep."

"Look," I said, "this isn't working. You're not giving me anything."

That's when he rolled over and said, "I'm attracted to another woman."

I remember getting out of bed with my big belly and saying, "What did you just say?"

"We need to talk. I'm attracted to another woman."

"We don't need to talk."

There had never been a divorce in my family. Despite all the pain and hardship we'd been through as a couple, I never would have divorced him. But when he cheated on me, I knew that was it. "I'm out of here."

I packed a bag for Zack and me. I called my sister, Kim, and she drove me to my parents' house in Cedar Falls. My son and I moved into my old high school bedroom.

The next day, I learned that "she" was nineteen years old and worked nights with Neil. He called me, trying to work it out, and I remember him specifically saying, "She doesn't tell me to take the garbage out. And she doesn't fight with me about money."

I was eight months pregnant and thinking, *Are you kidding me?* But I was done, so it really didn't matter what he said. It really didn't matter to me if he'd slept with her or not. To this day, I don't know whether he did or didn't. That surprises some people, but to me an affair doesn't have to be physical.

Did I cry?

Yes.

I cried a lot over those next few days and weeks. But remember, I'm a Marine. We're taught to take the hill before us and conquer the enemy. I had one child who depended on me and one on the way. So I kept moving, regardless of the obstacles. It wouldn't be until years later, when I was married to Kurt, that I would find out just how deeply I'd been wounded.

Flash forward nine months. I was divorced and the mother of two kids. Zack, my two-year-old with special needs, was eating Cheerios at the kitchen table. Jesse, who was eight months old, rode on my hip. I stood in the kitchen of my parents' house, wearing my mom's pink terry cloth bathrobe. I'd gotten up to feed the kids breakfast. My hair was a mess, and I still wore what was left of my makeup from the night before. I was a single mother on food stamps. The last thing on my mind was a relationship with a cute guy from the bar.

But Kurt had seen me open the blinds, and he knocked again.

CHAPTER 3

make out or
argue about Jesus?

{ KURT }

When Brenda opened the sliding glass door that day and I met the kids for the first time, I had no idea that one day they'd be *my* kids. After wrestling all night with her comment "I'll understand if I never see you again," I just wanted to put myself in the midst of it all and see how it felt. I might have left her house thinking, *Oh my gosh, are you kidding me? Not a chance!* But I'd rather know that up front than figure it out after five or ten dates.

I'm sure Brenda thought the opposite. She probably would have preferred if we'd gone out on a few more dates and then dressed up the kids nice and met at a restaurant where they would behave perfectly.

She would have told you that she wanted to protect her kids from another "cute guy." But I think at that time, and maybe still today, she wanted to protect herself from another guy who might cheat on her. Her first marriage had damaged her self-esteem and her ability to trust. Those issues are still alive in our marriage today.

I understand that now. When a coach says he'll give me a fair tryout, I want to trust him, but my experience has made me skeptical. My experience has taught me that for one reason or another, coaches don't always choose quarterbacks based on ability. Over time, I've grown as doubtful of coaches as Brenda had become of men. But that was all yet to come.

As I stepped into her parents' kitchen, I thought, *Good, I caught her off guard.*

She didn't have that perfect "Ladies Night" appearance I'd been so used to seeing. This was the real Brenda—messy hair, worn-off makeup, and disheveled robe. The question for me was, could I handle *real*? Could I deal with all this? If not, there was no reason to move forward, at least not romantically. But it wasn't Brenda who answered that question for me; it was her kids.

Zack back then was so much like Zack is now. He was just looking for somebody who would do what he wanted to do, who would make what was important to him important to them. And then—like now—radios were all he could talk about. He was fascinated with them. From the moment I stepped into the house, Zack took my hand and led me to every bedroom that had an AM/FM radio or an alarm clock. We talked and goofed around while Brenda—as she later told me—freaked out in the living room.

Of course she did. I'd shown up unannounced. She wasn't ready to see me, and she certainly wasn't ready for her special-needs child to give me a tour of her parents' house.

After the radio tour, Zack and I talked and played in his room. We even wrestled a bit. When we came back out, Brenda heard him call me "Mark." That was the name of the guy Brenda had been dating. She was embarrassed, but I loved it.

Jesse was only nine months old, and she was sitting on the floor. Brenda was sitting on the couch, but I got down on my belly so I could look Jesse in the eye while I played with her. She was a cute kid. But unlike Zack, who endeared himself to me so quickly, Jesse wanted nothing to do with me. It was months before she'd let me hold her.

The thing was, I'd always loved kids. Brenda's kids drew me in, and even now I tell her I fell in love with her kids first. But I also fell in love with Brenda being a mother to her kids. Usually, you don't know how someone will love your kids until after you're married. With Brenda, I got to see it from day one.

We talked a lot that day. I told her I was twenty-one and that I played football. I found out she was twenty-five and entering nursing school. And that she wasn't much of a football fan. As we talked, I began to appreciate the rare opportunity I was getting.

Growing up, I had chased a cheerleader or two. I'd pick out a cute one and then pursue her. But once I had her, it was never what it was cracked up to be—what you saw was all there was. With Brenda, from the first night I danced with her, I knew there were more layers to discover. That morning at her house confirmed two things: The kids were not a deal breaker, and I was more interested in Brenda than ever.

We continued to see each other at the bar, and we went out on a few dates. But neither of us had much money, so most of our dates were hanging out with the kids and ordering Domino's pizza. We'd eat dinner, put the kids down for bed, and then make out or argue about my religious beliefs.

I preferred making out—and we did a lot of it—but she still wanted to talk religion. Brenda and Neil hadn't agreed on faith issues, so it was important to her that we did. It wasn't that I was opposed to it; I grew up in the Catholic Church and still went to Mass occasionally. I knew it was something I should do more of, and I did it when I could; but unlike Brenda, I wasn't reading my Bible, going to Bible studies, or anything like that.

Brenda would tell you that I was a good person and I lived my life right. I wasn't into the things that other college guys my age were doing, so I thought I was pretty good. I couldn't understand why it was so important to her that I say a certain prayer.

Something would come up on TV or in a conversation, and I'd comment on it. Then she'd start in with the questions.

"Why do you believe what you believe?"

"I don't know."

She wanted me to say I believed certain things because they were in the Bible, but I honestly didn't know what was in the Bible. When I shared a belief or an idea, she would respond with, "Where in the Bible does it say that?"

And I'd think, *Shut up, let's make out.*

What was important to me was football, and while we were dating, I had opportunities to try out for NFL teams or demonstrate my skills for scouts that were visiting local teams. But whenever I had a shot at the pros, I didn't make it quite far enough in the evaluation process to achieve my dreams. For example, the summer after I graduated from college in 1994, I was invited to the Green Bay Packers' training camp. I made it through five weeks of workouts but was cut before the start of the season. I got a $5,000 check, and I used the money as a down payment on a green GMC Jimmy.

Prior to the Jimmy, I'd never owned a car. Brenda and I had shared hers, but all she had were $500 clunkers that she drove for a few months until they couldn't run anymore. There was one that only made left turns. It died when you turned right. One had rats in it, so you'd have to hit the dashboard to get them to be quiet; they'd scurry around underneath the seat and in the engine area. Another car wouldn't go up hills and left me stranded when I did an appearance at a local elementary school. The cars weren't great, but they were all we could afford.

So that's why the used-but-new-to-me green Jimmy was such a big deal. Finally, a car of my own—a car we could rely on. We could keep that car for years instead of months.

One cold winter night, while the four of us were going somewhere in the Jimmy, we ran out of gas on a desolate highway. We had no money. Brenda and I had to feel underneath the seats and the mats to get as many quarters and dimes as we could find. I got out and left Brenda and the kids in the cold car so I could walk to the nearest gas station to beg for some gas.

As I walked along that dark road, I thought, *What am*

I doing? I had been chasing my football dreams, but in doing so, I had followed a road of poverty that had literally left Brenda and the kids stranded on some lonely shoulder. I couldn't imagine what Brenda was thinking. She'd always been supportive of my dreams, but now she and the kids were watching their breath freeze while I was off begging for fuel.

As I carried the full gas can back to the car, my gloveless hands burned from the cold. *Something's got to change. All I'm doing is mooching off my girlfriend's parents while I pursue my dreams, and I can't even afford the gas to get back to their house.*

After that, I started working nights at the local Hy-Vee grocery store. I wanted to contribute something to Brenda's family while I continued to pursue my football dreams, so during the day, I watched Zack and Jesse. When Brenda or her parents got home, I would go work out with the Northern Iowa football team, just in case a scout came through. After that, I would come home and try to sleep for a couple of hours before reporting to work stocking shelves at the Hy-Vee. I was exhausted, but I felt good knowing I was finally able to help out Brenda and her family.

The job didn't cover all our needs, but it allowed me to buy gas for the Jimmy. It wasn't long, though, before I would have given that vehicle away if I could have.

When Zack was in preschool, he got a pencil injury to his head. It wasn't serious, but it did require a trip to the emergency room and some stitches. While he was there, they gave him some medication to numb the spot where they sewed him up. The medication apparently didn't agree with him, because on the way home, he projectile vomited all over the Jimmy. If you've never seen a child vomit like that, let's just say it was like watching an alien open its mouth and roar chunky, salmon-colored puke all over my prized vehicle. I didn't know whether to grab a tissue and start wiping it off the upholstered seats or off Zack. The vile smell overpowered us. We had to open the windows just to keep from gagging—or worse, vomiting ourselves. The chunks went in the vents, the sun visor, and the cracks in the seats. For as long as we owned that Jimmy, we could still smell the remnants.

Moments like that made me wonder if that was what I wanted and who I wanted to be. I loved Brenda and the kids. And looking back now, I realize those episodes taught me a lot. But at the time, I would rather have been learning from a coach than from a kid. I was young; did I want to have an instant family? And how would they affect my chances to play in the NFL? I didn't know the answer to that.

The Arena Football League had called me several times after I'd graduated, but I wasn't interested at first. At that time, arena football wasn't seen as a career path to the NFL. But in 1995, they were holding tryouts in Des Moines the same day that Brenda had to go there to take her nursing boards. If I tried out, we'd get two free nights in a hotel, and that seemed like a deal.

I tried out and did well. When they offered me a position on the Iowa Barnstormers, I decided to accept it. Taking the opportunity felt like a bit of a compromise. Although it paid better than stocking cans, I feared I might get injured or otherwise ruin my chances of getting an opportunity to play in the NFL. But at least I could play football again.

{ BRENDA }

April 14, 1996, was a Sunday, and the Sunday Night Movie had just ended. The movie was a little thing I'd do with my mom—she watched it in Arkansas where she and Dad had retired, and I watched it in Iowa. When the movie ended, she'd call and we'd talk about it and catch up on the kids or whatever was happening in our lives.

When the phone rang, I was surprised that it was my sister, Kim.

"Kim, I've got to let you go. Mom will be calling. The movie just finished."

In a soft voice, she said, "Sweetheart . . ."

I thought that was odd. We had come back from Kim's house in Eldridge earlier in the day, and Kim and I had been fighting.

But she repeated the word. "Sweetheart . . ."

There was a long pause, and I could tell she was trying to figure out what to say next. "About two hours ago, a tornado hit, and Mom and Dad were both killed."

"No!" I screamed. "No!"

I couldn't stop screaming. The kids were in bed asleep. Kurt was two hours away in Des Moines, where he was playing arena football. I hung up on Kim and called Kurt. "Kim called. Mom and Dad were just killed. Get here!"

My parents had just died, and at the moment I felt most

alone, there was no one I wanted to have with me more than Kurt.

+ + +

When I met Kurt in 1993, he was different from the other men—mostly Marines—I was used to. He didn't have the same discipline in the way he stood, dressed, or spoke. But he had a fluidity, a charisma about him that attracted people. And he had a childlike playfulness. In fact, the first time he told me he loved me, he wrote the message on a Magna Doodle, one of those write-and-erase toys.

We were just hanging out at the house, and Kurt was playing on the floor with the kids like he always did. Zack had the Magna Doodle, but he couldn't yet write words, so they were just messing around, drawing together. Then Kurt wrote, "I love my mama," and drew a little flower. Underneath that he wrote, "I love her too." Then he had Zack walk it over to me.

From the corner of my eye, I could see he was watching me read it. I looked up, and his brown eyes locked with mine. He had put himself out there, and I could tell he was holding his breath, waiting to see how I'd respond. I scribbled on the Magna Doodle and asked Zack to take it to Kurt.

Kurt read what I'd written: "I love my mama, too."

I knew he was disappointed, but I just wasn't ready to trust again.

Neil had left deep wounds on my soul. Like a good Marine, I'd built protection around myself to prevent further casualties. About Kurt, I thought, *This is fun, but you're not getting in. So let's go dancing. Let's hang out. Let's be the cute couple. You help me take care of my kids. You be another person that loves my kids and gives me a little bit of a break. You're filling up my life, but you're not getting in.*

And, like Neil, Kurt wasn't a believer. He was the best person I'd ever met. He didn't lie, he didn't swear, he didn't steal—he didn't do any of the major sins. He was such a good person. Good to everybody. And I'd think, *You're living a Christian life, Kurt. You're just not a Christian.* But I didn't want to marry another nonbeliever. So we got stuck on the "unless you pray for Jesus to come into your life, and ask him for forgiveness, you're not going to heaven" part. Over and over we'd argue about it. "It's not a religion," I'd say. "It's a relationship." I'd show him Scripture verses like John 3:3—"Unless you are born again, you cannot see the Kingdom of God."

He'd ask questions like, "What's 'born again'?"

And I'd tell him, "Well, that means you start over."

It just wasn't a big deal to Kurt, so eventually we'd stop talking and start making out.

Neil never did get saved while we were together, and seeing how that had worked out, I knew in my heart I couldn't commit to Kurt until he could commit to Jesus.

But Kurt *was* special, and he proved it to me about six months after we started dating. From the time Zack entered preschool, he'd always had special needs. Though he was mobile and could get around just fine, being legally blind made it hard for him to navigate around unfamiliar places. He also continued to require physical therapy.

The public school system offered many of the therapies he

needed, but to get those services, I was required to meet with his teacher and school administrators to create an Individual Education Plan, or IEP. I hated IEP meetings, and I probably whined about them a lot. One day, Kurt graciously and surprisingly said, "Do you want me to come to the next one?"

I wasn't sure. I mean, yes, I wanted the company, and it would have been great to have Kurt there. But I also thought, *This will lose him for sure.*

We arrived together for the meeting, and as soon as we walked into the classroom, I realized there would be a problem. The only chairs were the ones the kids sat in, and Kurt is six foot two. But that didn't stop him. As he introduced himself to the teacher, he pulled out a plastic chair and squeezed into it. During the meeting he oohed and aahed over Zack's finger painting. He asked intelligent questions when specific goals were discussed, and as the meeting went on, I could feel the room change from icy cold to warm and nurturing.

That's when I thought, *Doggone it, I love this guy.*

But were we marriage material? We had different spiritual beliefs, and he came from a divorced family. I already knew Kurt would be a great dad; I just didn't know whether he was the husband I needed.

I earned my nursing degree and found work at a nursing home in Cedar Falls, where the kids and I moved into government-supported housing. Kurt had an apartment in Des Moines, paid for by the Barnstormers. We were two hours apart, but we managed to get together on weekends, when the kids and I would go to his games, or he'd come up and stay with us during his off days.

Kurt did well in the Arena Football League. In his three seasons with the Iowa Barnstormers, he led the team to two Arena Bowl appearances and made the All-Arena team twice. He also joined a Bible study with some of the other players and started hearing some of the same things we'd been arguing about. The only difference was, he couldn't just stop and make out with them.

By now, we'd been dating for three or four years, and despite my trust issues, I started thinking that it was time for us to make a decision. We couldn't go on dating forever. I remember one conversation—it was typical of many we'd had.

"When are we going to make a decision about our future?" I asked.

"I don't want to get married until I have a job," Kurt said.

"But you do have a job with the Barnstormers."

"I want to wait until we have money in the bank. I don't know where all this is going."

"What are you waiting for? God to hit you over the head with a two-by-four so you'll know for sure?" It was a question I often asked him. His answer was always the same: "I hope he does."

But the truth was, Kurt wasn't ready, and sometimes he wasn't sure he ever would be. At the time, he didn't realize that you can't just put your life on hold until you have money in the bank or the perfect job. Relationships are what matter; the other stuff will come. But Kurt had his own dreams, and as much as he loved me, I know there were times he had to think, *I don't know if this is going to work.* His career was important to him, but I knew he also struggled with thoughts that maybe playing in the NFL would never happen.

Some days it was hard for me to trust that he would stick around. I'd get to the point where I'd think, *I'm done. I'm out of here. If you don't know whether I'm the one yet, then you never will.* But I couldn't make a clean break from him. It was as if every country song I heard at that time related to my poor, broken heart. I would listen and think, *Oh, I love that man. Doggone it. I'm not walking away. I'm not.*

But we did break up a couple of times. Once when he thought the turf would be greener with someone else. He was getting some attention because of football, and he got all full of himself. It took him about a week before he figured out that wasn't what he wanted.

There was another time when he attended a bachelor party for a friend of ours. Strippers performed at the party, and when I found out, I told Kurt I was done—and I meant it. I'd been cheated on once before, and though Kurt didn't do anything, the fact that he was even at the party was enough for me to end it. And so I did.

The next day, the kids were in the friend's wedding. I was miserable at the reception and spent most of my time trying to refill my punch glass without running into Kurt. After watching what was going on, my mom leaned across the table and said, "You never forgave Neil. Why don't you try to forgive just once in your life?" Then she and Dad left the reception with my kids and left me without a way home.

"Do you need a ride?" Kurt offered.

During that car ride home, he learned just how green with

jealousy I could get. I don't know if *jealousy* is even the right word. Protective. I didn't want the man I loved to even be in a situation where he could cheat on me. Of course, Kurt never did cheat. But when a burned heart gets close to fire, alarm bells go off that other people don't even know exist. We didn't know it then, but even now, a dozen years later, Kurt still has to douse the flames of jealousy from time to time.

Not long after that, my parents retired to Mountain View, Arkansas, where they built a house. We had lots of family down there, and that's where we'd spent all our vacations while I was growing up. Dad loved to fish, so his quaint cabin along the river was a dream come true.

Now Dad and Mom and their cabin were gone.

My parents were the two people I trusted most. They were my biggest cheerleaders, and I couldn't imagine life without them. I don't know how long I cried after Kim's phone call, but Jesse heard me and came walking into the kitchen in her little footed pajamas. I grabbed her and hugged her as hard as I could.

"Momma, whatcha crying about?"

At that point, I completely lost it. I screamed, howled, sobbed, whatever words you want to use. About then, people started showing up at my house. Family and cousins. Kim must have called them and had them check on me, but I remember thinking, *What are you people here for? My parents just died.*

It didn't take Kurt two hours to get there; he was much quicker. Because I was such a mess, he just stepped up and took care of the kids.

"Your mom's crying because she misses your grandma and grandpa. They loved you so much."

He could say for me what I wanted to say but wasn't capable of putting into words. He probably did more to help them with their grief than I did. How do you help your child when you're the child who's going through it? Something inside of Kurt just turned on. He'd never been through something like this either, but instinctively, he seemed to know just what to do and what to say.

The funeral took place in Arkansas. After the church service, Kim's husband, John, drove Kim, Kurt, and me to spread Mom's and Dad's ashes in a stream near their cabin. Kim and I each carried a black box of ashes on our laps. After we arrived, Kim and John started toward the water, but I stayed back. I wanted to talk to Kurt.

"Listen," I snapped at him, "if you're not going to marry me, it's really dumb that you're here right now!"

I know he thought I was crazy. A few minutes earlier in the van, I had looked at my box and then at Kim's and asked, "How do we know who is who?" We both laughed so hard; we hadn't been able to stop for miles. When it got quiet, one of us would start thinking about it again and the boys would hear, "Hmmm, Hmmm, Hmmm," until we exploded in giggles again. Kurt and John were appalled that we were laughing so hard; they didn't see anything funny about the situation.

But as I stood there now, looking Kurt in the eye, he knew I wasn't laughing anymore. I was serious.

"This is a lifetime memory thing, Kurt. So if you're not

going to stick around, it's stupid that you're here." Then I turned and walked toward Kim and John at the stream.

Kurt came with me.

+ + +

After my parents died, I moved to Des Moines to be closer to Kurt. I actually moved into the apartment he shared with another player. During this time, Kurt was the only one who let me continue to grieve as long as it took. He didn't quote Scripture or tell me it was for the better. He let me be angry with God and say whatever I wanted to say. And he would be mom and dad to my kids when there were times I couldn't be.

I know he also was grieving during this time. He knew and loved my parents, and when they were killed so suddenly, it was traumatic for him—though in a different way. I think it reintroduced so many of the questions about eternity that we'd discussed before.

One night, he came home and told me, "I prayed the prayer."

That was it.

At first, I thought he didn't really understand what it meant to confess his sins and claim Jesus as his Savior—mostly because he just kept talking. But over the next few months, I saw subtle changes in him. This was one of the lowest points of his life. My parents had died, so he was dealing with that, and he'd been benched from his starting position on the football team. Yet there was a sense of peace about him. He was baptized in the nasty lake water near where we lived.

It seemed that his heart had also softened toward the idea

of marriage. Looking back, I think Kurt had respected me enough to know he shouldn't ask me to marry him until his faith issues were worked out. It wasn't long after that, in September 1996, he proposed. He became my husband when we married in October of the following year.

At the wedding ceremony, the pastor presented us to the church as "Mr. and Mrs. Meoni," which was my last name from my first marriage. I still laugh about that—especially because, ever since that day, I've been referred to as "Kurt Warner's wife" rather than "Brenda."

After we were married, Kurt adopted Zack and Jesse, with permission from Neil, legally becoming what he already was—their dad.

CHAPTER 4

an introduction to the Warner rules

{ KURT }

Twelve years, four teams, three Super Bowls, and five more kids later, Brenda and I have finally figured out . . . that we'll never have it all figured out.

Three months after we got married, I spent a short season with NFL Europe playing for the Amsterdam Admirals. Being separated from Brenda, and my living in one of the most hedonistic cities in the world, was tough on both of us. But I knew the rules—I'd learned them after that bachelor party years earlier—and I also had a whole new set of rules that I imposed on myself because of my faith.

As a family, we moved to St. Louis when I started playing for the Rams. I led the team to two Super Bowl appearances, winning in 1999 and coming up short in 2001.

In 2004, I joined the New York Giants, and in 2005, we moved to Phoenix so I could play for the Cardinals.

People often ask us how we did it—three moves with seven kids, ups and downs in a high-profile career, and a marriage

that was thrust into the public eye. Our flippant answer is
that we didn't think about it. We just tried to survive each
day. But when we stop to think about it now, we recognize
that Brenda and I are very deliberate about these things. We're
intentional about how we run our house, how we raise our
kids, and how we love each other. And I think people pick up
on that and want to know more.

Recently, our family was profiled for an article in the *New
York Times*. While working on the piece, writer Karen Crouse
noticed that when we talked about the kids, we often referred
to "the rules." Right before deadline, she asked if the children
could come up with a list of rules for being a Warner kid.
They came up with eight off the tops of their heads. Here's
what was printed in the *New York Times*:

EIGHT RULES FOR BEING A WARNER DAUGHTER OR SON

1. *Everyone has to agree on which stranger's meal to pay for when dining at a restaurant.*
2. *At dinner, share the favorite part of your day.*
3. *Hold hands and pray before every meal.*
4. *After ordering at a restaurant, be able to tell Mom the server's eye color.*
5. *Throw away your trash at the movie theater and stack plates for the server at restaurants.*
6. *Spend one hour at an art museum when on the road.*
7. *Hold hands with a sibling for ten minutes if you can't get along.*

8. *If you can't get along holding hands, sit cheek to cheek. (If you can't get along cheek to cheek, then it's lips to lips!)*[1]

As parents, we were pleased that the kids not only understood we had expectations but also could articulate some of them. But the positive feedback we got from other people—family, friends, and complete strangers—surprised both Brenda and me. People wanted to know more about the rules, how we use them, and how they could use them in their homes.

That surprised us, because every family has its own set of rules. Some are simple: "Dad always takes out the garbage." Some are profound: "Put your spouse's needs before your own." I don't know that our rules are any simpler or more profound than any other family's. But I do know that with seven kids and a public career, we've had to become very clear about communicating and enforcing expectations for each other and for our kids.

In a fast-moving, chaotic household, having rules is a shortcut way of talking about those expectations. It sounds strict, like a lot of legalism, but it's not. The more we talked about our rules, the more we realized they were just our shorthand way of referring to a set of expectations. The rules aren't a hard-and-fast set of regulations carved in stone; rather, they're an easy way to refer to the checks and balances that keep our family together.

If our family is a team—and it often functions like one—the rules are just Team Warner's playbook. They're our guide to managing the chaos and not letting the chaos manage us.

But here's the thing: Some rules, like plays in football, are easier to understand in action than they are in the playbook. That's why, for the next few chapters, we won't give you a how-to manual about the Warner rules. Instead, we'll give you a glimpse into our lives and how the rules help us make it all work. Our hope is that maybe you'll find a few ideas that will work for your family and marriage—or at least a vocabulary you can use to talk about your own rules.

Join me now for a typical day with Team Warner.

In-Season Hours

One thing many people don't realize is that, even during the season, I'm around a lot. In fact, I probably get to spend more time with my kids than most parents who work nine to five are able to. It's a good gig.

During the season, I usually get up at five. I do a little cardio at the house and then leave for work. At the facility, I lift weights and watch some film. Usually, we have a team meeting around seven thirty, and after that it's practice. We meet again as a team after practice, and we're done somewhere around two or two forty-five. After practice on Wednesdays, we have Bible study, and on Thursdays we have a quarterbacks and receivers meeting. Most days, I'm home by four or four thirty.

As the week goes on, the days get shorter. Fridays, I'm usually home by one thirty, and Saturdays are just a short walk-through, so I'm only at practice for two-and-a-half hours. Saturday afternoons are free, so normally I'll go to one of Kade's games or Jada's cheerleading competitions.

I'm usually off on Monday or Tuesday, or I'll go in for only a few hours.

When I am home, I try to be fully present; just as when I'm on the field, I'm focused and prepared. That's one of my rules: Whether I'm with the kids or with my teammates, I always try to be in the moment.

Mornings at the Warner House

During the off-season, I sleep in till six thirty. I usually get up and get things going with the kids and let Brenda sleep longer since she has to get up early the rest of the year.

The first thing I do is wake up Zack. I pick out his clothes and lay them on the floor because he can't pick out his own clothes. He'll then dress himself. Usually, he gets his shirt on inside out or backward, so I'll help him when he gets to the kitchen.

Our kitchen is open and airy. There's a large Crate and Barrel farm table, where we eat, and a bar area with stools, where we keep the laptop. Because of the way the house is laid out, everyone must pass through the kitchen to get from one area of the house to another, so it's where everyone naturally gathers in the morning—dressed, not dressed, or half-dressed.

One of the rules at our house is that the kids can wear whatever they want. As Brenda says, "They won't wear that when they're sixteen, so why fight about it when they're seven?" When Jesse, our seventeen-year-old, was in elementary school, she'd wear every accessory she could find—all at once. A hat, earrings, multiple necklaces, and a scarf. This was when she was five or six years old. She was like a little Punky Brewster.

Another rule is that we encourage our kids to express their creative side, whether through the way they dress or in things such as art or music. Sometimes, parents unintentionally squash their kids' creativity by worrying too much about things that don't matter—like clothes.

In the hallway outside of the kitchen, we have a glass case. It's lighted from the inside and is meant to be a place to show off treasured collectibles. In ours, we keep the kids' school projects, pottery they've painted, or clay impressions of their handprints. There is even a statue of Belle from *Beauty and the Beast* that one of the kids painted. She's broken into about five pieces and rests inside a lopsided clay dish that another child painted. But we couldn't throw it away, because one of the kids made it.

I know many families display their children's artwork by hanging it in the playroom or on the refrigerator. But we want to celebrate our kids' creativity, so we frame it and hang it throughout the house. Right next to an expensive piece by a famous artist will hang a drawing that one of our children made at school. Anyone can do this. Brenda will tell you it doesn't cost much to buy a frame, put your child's art in it, and hang it on the wall, but what it does for your son or daughter is priceless. That's another rule for us: We celebrate creativity in all its forms.

Even in getting dressed.

The boys are so much easier. They couldn't care less. To make getting dressed faster, they'll wear just one color. Like this morning, Elijah was dressed in gray sweatpants and a gray V-neck shirt. Last week, Kade had on two different shades of red—one on his shorts and the other on his T-shirt. This morning, Kade's hair was all over the place, and he was like, "Yeah, I'm good." But Jada or Jesse? Neither one would ever walk out of the house without her hair done.

Breakfast is usually a bowl of cereal, a Toaster Strudel pastry, a bagel, or a Hot Pocket. The kids get their own food. Kade has three breakfasts. He eats a lot of food.

By now it's seven, and Brenda joins the rest of us in the kitchen. She checks the book bags while the kids brush their teeth. By seven thirty, everyone is at the bus stop, including the three-year-olds, Sienna and Sierra, wrapped in their robes or sweatshirts.

If Brenda is alone with the kids, as during the football season, she drinks her coffee while sitting on a special bench in the yard. It's made from the concrete steps that led to her parents' house, and it has her mom's and dad's handprints on the seat. It's one of the few things Brenda has that survived the tornado, and it's positioned where she can sit and watch the kids until the buses come.

When I'm home, I wait with the kids by the gate, and Brenda enjoys a minute of peace inside the house. But the kids love to annoy Brenda by pushing the intercom button on the gate. It makes the house phone ring and disturbs Mom's solitude.

Sierra will push it, Brenda will answer, and Sierra will say, "Whatcha doin'?"

We can hear Brenda laugh and say, "I'm drinking my coffee." And then she hangs up, and Sierra laughs.

Next, Sienna wants in on the action, so she pushes the button. When Brenda answers, Sienna will say, "Whatcha doin', Momma?"

Brenda laughs again. She's watching the whole thing on the security camera from inside the house. "I'm drinking my coffee, Babygirl." And then she hangs up.

Then Elijah pushes the button. "Whatcha doin', Momma?" By now, Brenda is getting annoyed, so that makes Kade and Jada want in on the action. Someone pushes the button, but there's no answer. By now, Brenda has taken the phone off the hook.

Later she'll say, "Why did you tell them to keep pushing the button?"

"They did it," I'll protest. "I didn't tell them to do it!" But I think she can tell from the security camera that it doesn't bother me the way it bothers her. "If you didn't keep hanging up, they wouldn't keep pushing it."

I think that's sort of an unspoken rule at our house. When someone gets annoyed with something we think is trivial, we continue to annoy them until we burn it out of them. That works for us because it usually makes the annoyed one laugh too.

After the kids are safely off to school, it's time for me to work out. Once I move the stuffed rabbit off my weights and the Little Tikes shopping cart off the treadmill, I can get some exercise. When we were in Hawaii for the Pro Bowl, I didn't work out for two days, and I just felt like, *Okay,*

I gotta go work out. I gotta go do something. It's hard for me to relax.

During the off-season, I spend a lot of time setting up schedules and preparing speeches. Through our First Things First Foundation, we participate in a variety of programs and put on an annual fund-raiser, so there's never a shortage of things vying for my time and attention.

The great thing about the off-season is that it is completely different from what I do during the regular season. So it's six months of one thing I love, and then it's six months of another thing I love. It's a great mix for me, because when I get tired of football, I can do something else, and when I get tired of that, it's time for football again.

{ BRENDA }

Kurt's description of our morning is just like him—focused. Reading it, you might think things always run smoothly and orderly—and for the most part they do. But with seven kids, there's often a lot of noise and confusion, especially as they're all trying to get their days started.

One morning, Elijah was complaining because he wanted his favorite football player's number drawn in frosting on his Toaster Strudel. I wrote *13* for Kurt. He wanted *11* for Larry Fitzgerald. So I tried to change it, but my *1s* didn't look like the numerals on the Cardinals jerseys, so he wasn't happy.

At least three kids will ask questions at once, and I only have two ears to hear and one mouth to answer. Someone will turn on the TV, and now some cartoon character is babbling away. I'll bump into the sharp corner of a drawer that somebody left open. The benches slide in and out, knocking against the table as each kid sits down or stands up. Kade will start making repetitive clinking sounds with the silverware against his bowl. By itself, each noise and activity isn't much, but when they're all together, our kitchen can sound like a junior high band without a bandleader.

And then there's Zack. Every morning when I go out to my car, I have to look underneath and behind each wheel, because he finds it fun to put things behind them. He likes the crunching sound they make when I back up. Sometimes it's a ball, a stick, or a can of soda. He wedges it right behind the tire, and because he can't see it, he thinks I won't see it either; he really thinks he's getting me, and he thinks that's funny.

But Zack also likes to have everything in its proper place. If there is a decorative pot on the floor, he thinks it should be on the table or the bookshelf. On one shelf, I have six decorative candleholders and a couple of vases. To properly display them, each item should be staggered with the ones on either side. But because Zack is so tactile, he likes to arrange them in straight rows so that they're all even. But I mess with him, because as soon as I see that he's straightened them, I go and stagger them.

As Kurt said, the kids are independent and get their own breakfast, but that also means someone eats food out of the dog bowl (that someone sent us for the puppy we never got). It means spilled milk on the table and cereal that gets crunched on the floor before it can be picked up. And that's another rule: Whether it's cereal on the floor or candlesticks in a row, we don't sweat the small stuff.

I don't have Kurt's ability to focus amid the chaos, and I need coffee to get my morning started. Even if I offered to get up first with the kids, Kurt wouldn't stay in bed. He can't stay down for long. He's a morning person *and* a night person. I'm a nap person. I don't have a peak-energy time of the day, so when he's home and offers to get up with the kids, I'm happy to take advantage of it. That's another of our rules: Those who are strong in one area help those who are weak.

Before the kids go to school, one of our morning rituals is to have them say the exact same four sentences they've said since their first day of school. The older ones know it by heart, but the little ones repeat it after me:

> *I'm the head and not the tail.*
>
> *I'm above and not below.*
>
> *I will find favor with man and God.*
>
> *I was created in the image of God*
> *to do good things and to love people.*

That's what we want to teach them: self-worth and that they have a God-given purpose. It sums up the basic philosophy we want our kids to live by: The head has a purpose, and they are here to serve others. If there's another rule here, it's that we try to find creative ways to frequently reinforce the things we consider important. This little recitation is one way we do it.

Saying those words was a big deal for Elijah, because he

just started saying them this year when he went to preschool for the first time. The Babygirls just repeat it after me. They're too young to think much about it other than it's a fun thing to do with Mom.

I used to be of the mind-set that, like the Bible says, "I can do all things through Christ who strengthens me."[2] Some Christian women focus on the Proverbs 31 woman. I focused on "I can do all things." But I've come to understand that just because I can doesn't mean I should.

I guess if I have a rule for running the house, it's to get good people I can trust and let them take care of things so that I can focus on what only I can do. We have people who come in and clean the house. Betsy, our full-time nanny, helps with the kids. But that doesn't mean the kids don't have things they're responsible for. Our rule is that the cleaning lady is here to clean, not to pick up after us, so each person is still responsible for his or her own mess. I can't tell you how great it has been for me personally, as a mother and as a woman, to have people who give me a break. I know I'm fortunate.

Speaking of breaks, I guess I should pick up the break in the schedule where Kurt left off.

Afternoons at the Warner House

On a typical afternoon, it might just be me and Babygirls at home. Elijah is at preschool on Mondays, Wednesdays, and Fridays. If Betsy is here, I might have lunch with some girl-friends or have a photographer friend come to the house and teach me more about photography. It's the first real hobby I've had since I became a mother. One thing I've done with my camera is take portraits of some of the sick children at the hospital where I go to hold babies. Many of the parents don't have pictures of their babies because they've been sick since birth. I wish now I had pictures of Zack when he was in the hospital.

Holding sick babies is something I enjoy doing. When I'm there, nobody knows or cares whose wife I am. It's just one way that I can give back; and now with Kurt's status, I've been able to ask other players' wives to join me as well. Kurt heard me talk about some of the babies for so long that he decided to come with me one day and got to see how much I enjoy loving on those babies.

At home, Kurt is just loving on the kids. They're hanging out in the game room or swimming in the pool. Sometimes, if they're all busy, I'll try to disappear for a while. Kurt and I both like to read and then discuss what we're reading. So if I get a chance to be alone—I am *never* alone—I like to escape for a few minutes with a good book. I also try to catch a yoga class; it's something that makes my back feel better, helps me stay in shape, and relieves stress.

It's funny; one of the things that we've had to learn about each other is that we both need different things. I need time alone, and I need time with my girlfriends. Kurt is less likely to take time for himself. We've had to learn to appreciate each other's differences, and I guess that's another rule: Respect each other's differences.

Evenings at the Warner House
Everyone comes home from school around three, and I can tell because the noise level immediately cranks up. The kids

are expected to do their homework and to ask for help if they need it.

At this point, I am usually trying to figure out a meal I can make that everyone will eat. With nine people, all with different tastes, it's not an easy task. Kurt likes meat, and Jada is a vegetarian, so I can never please everyone. Pasta is normally what you make for a crowd, but Kurt doesn't like pasta, so it's always a challenge to make the evening meal work.

The kids want to snack from the minute they get home, so we try to eat dinner around four thirty or five. We always eat dinner together as a family. That's one rule that's rarely broken. If the kids want to have dinner with their friends, they're welcome to bring them here. But they all have to be home for dinner.

We all hold hands and pray, and then someone will say, "Sienna, what's the best part of your day?"

She'll tell us something like, "Going to Little Gym." Then she will ask another child, and we do this until all the kids have told us about the best part of their day.

We try to make them give more than just a one-word answer like "recess." As far as we're concerned, this is story time, and it's their moment to step up and be the storyteller. We do this every single night. We used to do highs and lows, but the lows got to be such detailed accounts of things that one sibling did to another and caused bickering at the table. So we stopped asking about the lows. Of course, it's important for them to share those, too, but because it just kind of ruined dinner, we now just do the highs.

On birthdays, we always go around the table and tell our

favorite thing—what we love—about the birthday person. And the rule is that you can't say the same thing that somebody else has already said. So if Jada says she loves Zack watching cartoons with her, Elijah has to find something else he loves about Zack. This is such a simple thing that any family can do. But I think it helps the kids to see their own worth—and their worth through the eyes of their family. This can also be such an important bonding activity for our family. The kids are often surprised at what their siblings say, and they remember it long after the birthday dinner is over.

Dinner comes with lots of rules, such as no one may get up from the table until the last person is done eating. The boys can eat as fast as they want, but they have to stay at the table until their sisters are done. It's our way of telling the kids that each one is as important as all the others, and nothing is more important than our family time.

After dinner, everyone has a chore. Each kid knows what he or she is supposed to do. That's my number one dinner rule: If you cook, you don't have to clean up.

In the evening, there's usually time for a short movie. Everybody has to agree on the movie, and it has to be appropriate for the whole family. We want the kids to stay together and not to go to their rooms to watch TV alone. Sometimes we'll play Wii or a table game, like Uno, that all ages can play. On nights when the kids have activities, like soccer practice, we all pile into the big blue van and go together. I know that for many families, even those who eat dinner together, it's tempting for family members to scatter after dinner and do their own thing. But for us, evenings are a sacred time, a time when we can be together. So, as much as possible, we commit to doing things together as a family, even if it means we all have to go to one of the kids' practices or games.

Bedtime

The bedtime routine begins around seven thirty. Our bathroom shower is like an assembly line producing clean kids. We usually do showers every other day. Now that Kade is ten, he usually showers in his own bathroom. But Kurt will have Jada, Elijah, and Babygirls lined up in ours. He will squirt shampoo on one and say, "Okay, go over there and scrub." Then the next one in line, and so on. So it's shampoo, shampoo, shampoo, shampoo, then conditioner, conditioner, conditioner, conditioner—assembly-line style.

We don't often do baths, because we have only one tub and the kids just end up sitting in each other's grime. But sometimes they just have to be dunked. The other day, Kade's hair was funky; he hadn't showered in a few days, and his hair was full of styling gel. "We don't have time to give you a shower," we told him. "Jump in the pool and then go get dressed." Sometimes the quickest method is the best.

After showers, it's bedtime. All the kids put on their own pajamas—of course the tops never match the bottoms—and comb their own hair. Kurt helps the younger kids brush their teeth. Then we put them to bed. If Kurt's home, he prays with each child individually before bed. I go around and kiss everyone; it's my favorite time of the day because it's the only time my kisses don't get rubbed off. I get a lot of love at bedtime. They seem to like it, but then maybe it's because it prolongs their bedtime.

I know that all this might sound boring, but one of my rules is to find beauty in the daily rituals of life. It's my prayer that the kids will take these memories with them into their own families—where they will have the same memories.

CHAPTER 5

strive to be the best you can be

{ KURT }

The Cardinals were the worst team in NFL history. In their sixty-year existence, they'd never been to a Super Bowl and had played in only a handful of playoff games.

When we entered the 2008 season playoffs, no one expected much. We were 9–7. People called us the worst team ever to go to the playoffs. We were the underdogs in *every* game.

And yet we got to the Super Bowl.

We even had a chance to win it in the end.

When I was in St. Louis, the Rams were considered one of the worst teams of the nineties, yet in one year, we went from worst to first, winning the 1999 Super Bowl. In my years as a player, I've been a part of some real come-from-behind stories.

There have also been times in my career when I've had personal comebacks. There were times when I was benched through no fault of my own, and times when injuries prevented me from playing. Times when I did everything I could but still got booed coming off the field. Let me just say, it's never good when you're booed in your profession. Those were the low moments in my career. Moments when I would ask God, *What are you doing? Why am I here?*

I had some of those same questions when I was benched two years after coming to Arizona. I worried that my entire future as a player would be limited to holding a clipboard, just waiting to see if the starter got injured. I considered retirement in those days, but I also hoped that by working hard I could change the situation. Before I got into the NFL, I was naive. I believed the best players would always play because coaches wanted to win games. But once I got into the league, I learned it's also about other things—money, draft picks, politics, and marketing. But despite the low times—no matter how much the fans or coaches turned against me— I've always tried my best, and I will always continue to do my best.

That's what I want my kids to see.

Yes, I'm proud of my accomplishments. My quarterback rating is in the top five all-time, better than some of my heroes, like Joe Montana and Roger Staubach. I'm one of the most accurate passers in NFL history, which makes me happy because I believe that's my greatest strength. Throughout my career, there have been other accomplishments that have stood out, such as fastest to throw for ten thousand yards, sec- ond fastest to a hundred touchdowns, and second all-time to throw forty touchdown passes in a season—with my name in the record books alongside Dan Marino's. My stats are up there with some of the best ever to have played the game.

But beyond the statistics, I'm even more proud that I took two different teams to the Super Bowl. Regardless of the odds against me, or the accolades I've received, I've always done my best to be a leader on the field and to inspire other players to greatness. So, on the one hand, if my career ended today, I would be satisfied. But the truth is, I'm not done and there's more I want to accomplish. I want to become an even better quarterback. I want to throw more touchdown passes, break more records, and win more Super Bowls. I want to play the perfect game.

I'm not saying I want to accomplish these things so people will look at me and say, "Oh, he's the best quarterback that ever played," or whatever. I'm not really worried about what other people think or say. I just want to be the best I can be—to live up to my fullest potential. And I hope that in doing so, I inspire the people who watch me to be the best at what they're supposed to be.

After the Super Bowl, it would have been so easy to pick one of those two pivotal plays—the interception to James Harrison or the touchdown to Larry Fitzgerald—and have that define me. But those aren't the moments that play over and over in my head. The moments I relive are the conversations I've had with people who stopped to tell me that I inspired them.

For example, I remember one of my first years in Phoenix. Larry Fitzgerald and his girlfriend were having dinner with Brenda and me. Sometime during the main course, Larry and I got into a heated discussion about something related to football, and I said to him, "You've got to get better."

I'll never forget his response: "Kurt, I'm good enough."

Brenda was there, and she will tell you that I couldn't believe he'd said that. It blew me away that "good enough" would be okay.

"Don't you want to be the best?" I asked.

That conversation stuck with me. When I disagree with someone on a topic, I'm the kind of person who always asks a lot of questions—like, "Why do you believe what you believe?" I want to understand their thinking and how they arrived at the conclusion they did. That's what I did when Brenda and I were dating and she kept talking about religion.

That's probably also why I still remember that conversation with Larry. I had no idea why Larry would think it was okay for him just to be "good enough."

Over the next few years, Larry and I became pretty good friends. We worked closely together, both on and off the field, and I got to watch him grow from a good player into a great player.

After the Super Bowl, Larry and I were traveling together on a plane, and we had another conversation I'll never forget. He locked eyes with me and said, "Kurt, you made me better. You made me want to be better."

That's it.

That's what I live for.

I want my life to encourage others. Whether as the leader of a football team, as a husband to my wife, or as a father to my kids, I always strive to do my best in hopes that by doing so, the people around me will strive to do their best. I want a spirit of excellence to surround everything I do. When my kids see me loving them, when they watch how I treat my wife, or when they see me preparing for football, I want them to know that I'm doing my best. I also hope that pushes them to do better in what they're doing. I want to be great. And I hope to inspire others to want the same.

The Best Dad I Can Be

Some people believe that being a great dad means never raising your voice, treating all your kids equally, and always being there for them. If that's the case, I don't make the grade, because at one time or another I've failed at all those things. But it's not that simple.

I've come to learn that being a good parent is not about balancing my time perfectly. I don't try to make sure I give each kid the same amount of attention every day, every week, or every month. And I never say, "I spent seven hours on football today, so now I'm going to spend seven hours with the kids."

No matter how hard I try, I'm not always going to have a calm voice. I won't make all the right decisions with my daughters. And I'm not always going to go outside to play football every time the boys ask. So if that's what defines the perfect dad, well, then I'm not.

Still, when I'm with my kids, I try to stay focused on them. I want them to know that I care about them, love them, and am there for them no matter what they need. My goal is to be totally engaged; but there are times when I miss the mark, times when I come home from work with thirty-seven things on my mind and I can't just block them out.

However, even when I come up short, I want my kids to know I tried my best.

Even if I fail at focusing all my attention on the kids, I want them to know that my love is greater than my attention. When I tell my kids I love them, I'm not saying, "I'll do whatever you want me to do, all the time, and you'll be the center of my universe."

Sometimes loving my kids means loving my wife.

Sometimes loving them means excelling at my job.

Sometimes loving them means serving others because that's what God has called me to do. My love for Jesus overrides everything else in my life. I have to fulfill that call.

Those are the things that motivate my life: my love for God, for my wife, and for my kids. As long as my wife and kids know that I love them, I don't care if, at any given moment, I'm not the best father or husband by someone else's standards.

I want my kids to be able say, "Although he screws up, I know he loves me and wants to be a great dad."

I want them to say, "Although Mom gets mad and yells at him, I know he still loves her and wants to be a great husband."

And I want them to say, "I am proud of my dad because he tries to be great in everything he does," not, "I'm proud of my dad because he's an NFL quarterback."

I'm not perfect, but I continue striving to be the best I can be at the things I do. A lot of nights I go to sleep thinking, *I have to do better tomorrow*. But there are plenty of days when I can say, "I was a good dad today," or when one of the kids falls asleep in my arms and I think, *I'm doing what God has called me to do as a father*. Sometimes I step off the football field and think, *That was a special performance; I played well today.* And some of my favorite times are those moments when my wife looks at me and doesn't say anything but I can just tell I did well from the look on her face.

Occasionally, my kids show me that I am doing well, when I see them striving to do their best. Like Jesse. She's already been admitted to the college she wants to attend. She has every reason to blow off classes during the final semester of her senior year. She could just take a few fluff courses to mark time until graduation. The outcome wouldn't change much. But she's taking a full load of courses, including AP classes. Plus, she's involved in music and drama extracurricular activities. She recently told someone that she continues to push herself because she believes that God created her for something big and he's pushing her in new directions. She owes it to herself and to God to give it her best effort.

That's the rule, not only for my kids but for me—to continually strive to be all that we can be, to never settle for "good enough," and to enjoy the moments when we've done well.

{ BRENDA }

"Be all that you can be" may be a slogan for the Army, but it's also a philosophy this former Marine believes in and tries to live by. But that doesn't mean it's easy.

After I divorced Neil, I had a lot of anger and bitterness. As I said, I didn't know anyone who had ever been divorced, so there was no one to talk with about what I was feeling or a role model to emulate. The first divorced people I ever met were Kurt's mother and father. And though they are now married to other people and get along, when I first met them, they found it hard to say nice things about each other or even to be in the same room together.

I could understand their pain. One of the hardest things about the divorce for me was having Neil come to my parents' house to visit with Zack and Jesse. Though I wanted the kids to maintain a relationship with their father, it was sometimes painful to watch him have these happy little two-hour visits where everything was "perfect" while I had to work all week just to do the best I could.

Neil always brought his girlfriend, too—the same one he'd left me for. They would be on the floor playing with the kids, and I couldn't help but watch how the two of them interacted. As a woman who had been cheated on, I had a lot of unanswered questions: *What does he see in her? Is she really better than I am? Was she really worth breaking up our marriage and our family?*

Sometimes Neil would bring the kids new toys, and I would wish I could have done something like that. As a single mom on food stamps, I was always struggling to make ends meet. When I needed to buy my kids clothes and shoes, I didn't shop at the mall; I shopped at garage sales. There was never enough money for the basics, let alone the extras, so I could never buy the kids brand-new toys. I'd see them get excited about the gifts Neil brought, and I wished I could afford to do the same. But I couldn't, because I was the one buying their food.

I'm a passionate person, and I have no problem expressing my opinion. It would have been so easy to let loose with
my anger and say a few things to turn the kids against Neil.
If there was a fight for who was right and who was wrong, I
knew I could win the battle, because he was the one who had
cheated. I could say all the right things so that I would be
Zack's and Jesse's favorite. But I never did that. I never played
games with my kids or used them as pawns in a grudge match
against their father.

I had watched how horrible it was for Kurt when one
of his parents spoke negatively about the other, and I never
wanted to cause my kids that kind of pain. So my rule was
that I never said bad things about Neil. Instead, I was openly
supportive of him and did everything I could to encourage
my kids to have a good relationship with him.

It would have been so easy to stay angry, but letting go of
my anger wasn't just about doing the right thing for my kids.
It was about making me a better person. It strengthened me.
Sometimes, the toughest things we go through are the things
that change us the most—for better or for worse. My choice
was to change for the better. I didn't want to be a divorced
woman who was filled with anger and hatred toward her ex. I
wanted to be a loving mother to my kids. To do that meant I
had to be willing to let go of the fact that I was wronged and
instead concentrate on doing the right thing.

That experience made me better, but fortunately there are
some other, less painful things that I continue to do to be the
best I can be. For example, I love photography. And though
I've wanted to be a photographer since I was a young girl,

I think photography became even more important to me after my parents died. We recovered very little from their house—a few quilts and a box of pictures. But those pictures are priceless to me. I could look at one and remember tastes and smells that I hadn't thought about in years.

Those treasured pictures were a reminder to me that the photos I take are more than just images; they're a way of documenting my children's lives. Someday after I am gone, the pictures I take now will help them to remember their own childhoods. But that doesn't mean I'm content with just taking snapshots. I want to be the best photo documenter I can be. I want each picture I take to tell a wordless story. So I continually try to develop my skills by taking photography classes, having other photographers mentor me, learning new software programs, and studying famous photographers when I visit art museums with the kids. Recently, I've had a few of my photos published—in the *New York Times* and in a local magazine. I can't tell you the satisfaction that has brought me, knowing that my hard work is paying off.

Though both Kurt and I want to be the best we can be, there are times when we have different ideas of what it means to be our best. I've known Kurt for more than sixteen years, and though I can testify that he does his best at anything he wants to do, I have to be truthful and say the emphasis is on the "wants" part. If somebody else decides he ought to do something like—say—clean the house before company comes over, then he hates it. He hates it when I try to have the house nice for company. He says I try to make it too perfect. All I really want are clean hand towels in the bathroom, ones without toothpaste on them. I also think it looks pretty if the pillows are lined up on the furniture, the towels are folded, and the food is laid out nicely.

Kurt says it's not how we live on a daily basis. He's right, of course, but that doesn't stop me from trying to make the house the best it can be when people come over. That's one way I try to do my best.

A related rule is that sometimes you need to support other people in being their best, even if you don't care whether the hand towels have toothpaste on them. Kurt's usually great at helping around the house. On a normal day, by the time he gets home from work or traveling, and I'm exhausted, he's the one who steps up and helps take care of the kids or the house. But he's not happy when my need for greatness comes out right before company comes; he finds it stressful because the bar has been raised.

Even when we're all trying to do the best we can, in a large family there's always someone pulling you in a direction you'd rather not go.

Like the other night, Kurt and I were in bed and . . . uh, things were happening. Right in the middle of it, we heard Sienna yelling, "Daddy!" We tried to ignore her, but she kept yelling, "Daddy!"

I was thinking, *She's going to stop any minute.* And Kurt also thought she'd stop. But we have cathedral ceilings and everything echoes throughout the house—and she wouldn't be quiet.

Finally Kurt said, "I'm going to have to go down there." We both started laughing, because no matter how much we wanted to stay focused on each other, how could we stay in the mood with all that racket going on? It turned out Sienna wanted Kurt to push play on the DVD player, but to do that, he had to put me on pause.

So, although we both want to always be at our best, sometimes we aren't. Sometimes there are interruptions in life, and sometimes—just like some of the setbacks Kurt has faced on the field—life isn't fair.

Being Your Best When Life Isn't Fair

Several days before his games, Kurt gets into what I call "the zone." Though he's with us physically, we can tell he isn't there mentally. Sometimes I feel as if it's not fair that I don't get the good Kurt. But I know I also carry a lot of baggage from my first marriage. I find it hard to trust, and though Kurt has never given me a reason not to trust him, I still have issues. My first husband robbed me of the ability to place 100 percent trust in any man. That's not fair to Kurt, but those things are trivial compared to the issues others face when trying to be their best.

Like Zack.

He didn't ask for what he got in life. Being all that he can be not only is harder for him but also means different things than it does for our other kids. For example, when Jesse moves away from home, we know what her path will look like: college, maybe graduate school, and then a job. We don't know what Zack's path will look like when he leaves our house.

After Zack's accident, a doctor told me I'd be lucky if Zack could ever sit up. But that didn't stop me from hoping and praying for more. Zack and I worked hard at his therapy and rehabilitation in those early days, and it paid off.

When Zack was about two and a half, he learned to walk with a walker, which gave him the stability he needed. It was difficult to move around in the orthotic braces that wrapped around his legs and kept his toes from pointing out. The walker was like an old person's walker, but it was sized for a two-year-old. Zack also had a patch over his good eye to strengthen the weak one. He often got attention because he looked so cute as he walked with me.

I remember the last time he used the walker. It was while we were shopping at a Von Maur department store. We were walking past the escalators, which are located in the central area of the store, and there was a piano player entertaining the shoppers. Next to the piano was a bird cage. As we walked past, with Zack pushing his little walker, he heard the bird. Even at two he knew that birds didn't belong in that environment. Because he couldn't see the cage, he didn't know where the sound had come from, so he let go of the walker to go investigate.

That was the moment when I knew that Zack would be able to do things that the "experts" had said he couldn't. Although there was a lot of falling and stumbling yet to come, from that time on there was no more walker for him to hang on to.

As a parent, I always wanted Zack to grow up to be the best person he could be. But as the parent of a special-needs child, I also wanted to keep him safe. I'd always believed that God had a plan for Zack but that the plan had changed when he was injured. It occurred to me that by trying to protect him, I might keep him from doing what he was called to do. I knew then that my job wasn't to keep him safe so much as it was to help him fulfill his God-given purpose, even when it wasn't comfortable for me.

Fortunately, I'd had a great role model for that. Back in the early 1990s, my parents had an itty-bitty cabin on a lake near Harpers Ferry, Iowa, and the whole family would go up there on weekends. When Zack was as young as four years old, Dad would let him drive the boat and guide him by saying, "A little bit to the right now. Now back to the left." Though blind, Zack learned to steer the boat through my dad's commands.

Dad also gave Zack a fishing pole and taught him to fish. If Zack caught something, my dad didn't haul it out of the water for him; he made Zack do it. Dad let Zack feel the fish and get his hands all slimy.

There have been times when I've had to fight for Zack in order for him to reach his potential. We've always sent him to public schools, because that's what's best for his needs. The public school system has more money for special-needs students than private schools do. But everything they decide to do, or not do, is related to money, because what is spent on one kid is money that can't be spent on another. As a parent, your choices are either to roll over and sign off on whatever the experts say—even if you feel it's not enough—or to fight for your child.

You already know which option I chose, don't you?

For sixteen years now, I've fought to get Zachary what he

needed, but I've also worried about parents who didn't know how to fight or who gave in to people who were considered experts and thought they knew what was best.

When Zachary was little, the experts wanted to label him as retarded. But he wasn't. I also hate that word. Though I realize it was a medical diagnosis, it's also a negative and hurtful word. At our house, I don't let the other kids say it; they call it the "*R* word." I was afraid that if the doctors attached that word to Zack's record, they would give up trying with him, or they'd feel as if they didn't have to work as hard to teach him. I didn't want the *R* word on his file, because he had already proved that he could do so much more. The experts said, "Well, we need to put *something* on his chart so when we grab it we'll know who he is."

And that was exactly why I didn't let them do it.

Special needs or not, I think one of the worst things we can do is label our children. I grew up always thinking my sister was "the smart one" and I was "the pretty one." It wasn't until I was in the Marines and tested high for intelligence that I realized maybe I was smart too. That's why I try to avoid labels as much as possible. Labels can prevent us from becoming our best selves.

Zack is now in his third senior year, and he's nineteen. He can stay in public school until he's twenty-two, and we're also working on teaching him some job skills. It's hard to imagine him not living with us, but ultimately that's what everyone wants for their child, their grown child. As much as it scares us, we also know that it's best for Zack.

I like Kurt's approach of always trying to be the best you

can be. Just like with the walker, it helps me realize that some-times when I'm too protective, I actually hold my kids back from achieving their potential. Sometimes, achieving your best means you fall, get hurt, or get benched on the way to greatness; but you still pick yourself up and give it your best the next time. That's what true greatness is. I'm grateful that my kids live with a role model who does that every day.

CHAPTER 6

parenting differences

{ KURT }

Though Brenda and I are a couple and stand united on the big things, we each have our own individual characteristics as well. For example, Brenda loves the sun, and I don't. The last time we were on vacation, she lay in the sun while I hid under an umbrella at the cabana.

When we go out to eat, I like meat and she likes vegetables.

At the movies, the Marine in her loves shoot-'em-up movies. She says I like girlie movies.

I try to see the good in everything. Brenda is more skeptical. And when it comes to the kids, she hates it when they want to play with her iPhone. "It's not a toy," she tells them. I'm just the opposite. I hand them mine and tell them to have fun.

One of our biggest differences is in how to handle fans when they come up and want me to sign something. It's supposed to be a rule that I don't sign when I'm with my kids—my focus is on them. So Brenda believes that when someone asks, I should use that as a teaching opportunity and explain that the reason I don't want to sign is that I'm with my kids. She thinks it will prevent them from doing it to someone else in the future. I, on the other hand, think the fan doesn't care; it's just faster to sign it and be done.

Those are trivial differences, and they don't matter much. But we also recognize that there are big differences in our personalities, in our past experiences, and in our relationships with family and friends. We don't see these differences as negatives. In fact, we recognize and honor them because they make us stronger as a couple and as parents.

Our kids notice those differences too. If you asked Jesse, she would tell you that her mom has a low tolerance for repetitive noises. Jesse's not fond of those either, but with young kids in the house, there is always a clatter going on somewhere. One of the kids will be clanging toys together right in front of me, and Jesse and Brenda will say to each other, "How can he read a book with all that racket?" I don't know how, but I can.

Jesse also notices differences in our parenting styles. She would describe Brenda as "superstrict." With me, she would say that although I'm tough on the field, I'm a pushover at home. She has even affectionately called me a wimp. Recognizing that difference, she's quick to take advantage of it. When she wants to spend the night at a friend's house, she'll try my cell phone before she'll call the house phone. She knows I'll probably say yes before Brenda will.

Jesse's not the only child who recognizes the differences and tries to use them to gain an advantage. At three, the twins already know whose buttons to push—usually mine—to get what they want. The joke is that if I ran the house, the kids could do whatever they wanted, and they would run wild. But fortunately, Brenda is there, and she's always on the ball, keeping things in order. Though she may be more strict, she also has the maternal instinct.

Ultimately, we think our differences work for the good of the family. They allow us to find balance in our parenting. Of course, when there's a major issue with one of our children, Brenda and I have to be in agreement. One can't say yes and the other no. But otherwise, like in any good marriage, our differences work to complement each other.

The same is true of our kids. Each has special gifts and talents, and their unique interests fill different roles in our family.

When the kids are working on homework that requires some creativity, we always say, "Go get Jesse, and have her help you."

Kade is very compassionate. He's a funny guy, always bringing humor to our family.

Jada is an organizer; she's the one who keeps it all together. She is always clean, dresses nicely, and keeps her room tidy.

Zack is never demanding. He'll serve the other kids and never ask for anything for himself.

Elijah is really into sports, and he always wants to do whatever his big brother Kade is doing.

Even the twins, Sienna and Sierra, have slightly different roles. Sienna has a sweetness, a softness about her, whereas Sierra is like her mom, short and spicy. She has an edge and a fire. She doesn't back down from anything, even though she's the smallest one. Each of our kids reminds us of something, whether it is our own limitations, our desire for humility, or just the pleasures to be found in the simple things of life. I can't imagine life without any one of them.

I often hear parents comparing one child to another: "Why don't you get good grades like your sister?" or "Why can't you behave like your brother?" I don't want my kids to be just like their siblings. I want to celebrate their unique qualities, share their interests, and help them develop their own gifts—no matter what that looks like.

Take Zack. For whatever reason, he likes to pick up things around the house. He cleans up the yard when the kids leave their riding toys out. He can't sleep at night knowing they aren't put away, so after everyone is done playing, he will go out, pick up all the toys, and put them in the garage. If the throw pillows from the couch have been tossed on the floor, Zack will pick them up. Brenda has some floor decorations, like oversized vases or pottery, around the house, but Zack will put them on a shelf in neatly organized rows.

Lately his interest in picking up has expanded outside the house. His favorite thing is to pick up trash. It gives him purpose. We'll be out somewhere in public, and if Zack steps on a wrapper or something, he'll stop to pick it up. He collects garbage—bottle caps, used napkins, candy wrappers, whatever he finds—picking it up and putting it into his pocket until he can find a trash can. Some days, Jesse will see him on the bus and his arms will be full of bark that has fallen off palm trees or some other debris. He's just holding on to it until he gets to school, where he can throw it away.

During the football season, Brenda takes each of the kids individually on a special weekend to see one of my away games. After their weekend, they'll come home and talk about what they did, who they saw, or where they ate. Zack won't talk about any of those things. He'll talk about how happy he was that he and Brenda walked a mile to a museum, picking up trash the whole way. And how after they spent an hour at the museum, he got to pick up trash on the other side of the street as they walked the mile back to the hotel.

Picking up trash is not my thing. It's not Brenda's thing. And certainly none of our other kids would volunteer to pick up trash. But when you see the joy that Zack gets from doing it, well, you just want to help him do more of it. As Zack's parents, we've tried to let his interests lead us into new directions and then use those interests to expand or broaden his world. So, if picking up trash in parking lots and vacant lots helps him learn more about contributing to the world around him, we try to follow his lead and then capitalize on it for teaching purposes.

Our other children have unique interests as well. Jesse, for example, is an artist and a musician. She has beautiful charcoal drawings littering her room, and though she doesn't see their worth, we recognize her artistic talents. She taught herself piano and guitar, and she can sing. Oh, how she can sing! When she's performing in an ensemble or a musical, it's easy to see the joy it brings her. Although you'll never catch me singing the national anthem before thousands of people at a Cardinals game, I get great joy from watching Jesse celebrate her talents in front of an audience. When Zack picks up trash and when Jesse performs, they each feel as if they have purpose and meaning in what they do.

Brenda and I love seeing our kids' individual differences, but their differences also require us to parent them in unique ways. For example, Kade is as competitive as I am. He tries to make everything a game, just so he can win it. And he hates to lose. Did I mention he's just like me? Last year wasn't a very good year for him. He was on a Pop Warner football team that didn't win many games. Kade would have to get up very early on Saturday mornings to go play, and he'd mope around the house saying he didn't want to go.

"You're the one who wanted to play. You signed up for this," I'd remind him. "We have to go. Everybody's counting on you."

"I just don't want to play another game where we don't score any points," he'd say. "We're so bad, and I don't want to lose."

How do you parent that?

My job is to win football games. That's what I am paid to do, and it has taken me years to learn how to deal with winning and losing. For Kade, it shouldn't be about winning and losing; it should be about having fun. But with a kid as competitive as he is, you can't just tell him to get over it.

One way I tried to help Kade was by setting aside some special time with him on game days. We'd get up while it was still dark outside and go to McDonald's. Together we'd relax and talk over Egg McMuffins. It was just a little thing we did that helped him to focus on our time together rather than on the expected final score. Kade needs us to help him refocus on the bigger picture.

I've also tried to take the competitive pressure off Kade by carefully choosing my questions after the game. I don't ask about his performance. Instead, I ask if he had fun. This is not a kid that you motivate by increasing the pressure—he already puts enough pressure on himself. But there are also times I can use his competitive side to help him achieve things. Like when he does chores. All I have to do is time him or make a game out of it, and he forgets that it's a chore. His competitive nature serves him well in those moments.

Jesse, on the other hand, doesn't have a competitive bone in her body. So, just to have fun with her, I challenge her at American Idol on the Wii. I'm not bad, but Jesse is better. She's beaten me every time, and I think it gives her a thrill to see me lose. She knows that, like Kade, I hate to lose. But secretly, I also enjoy watching her develop a competitive streak.

Because of those differences, Brenda and I have to vary how we parent each child. But because she and I also have differences in personality, those differences spill over into our parenting styles. And sometimes we disagree with each other's approach. Like the time I taught Zack how to drive.

Parenting outside the Bubble

For as long as I can remember, Zack's one desire has been to drive. He used to tell everyone that he wanted to be a black truck driver. Of course, what he meant was that he wanted to drive a black truck.

"I can't wait until I'm sixteen so I can drive," he'd tell us.

We never said that he couldn't. At that time, sixteen was

a long way off, so telling a blind boy he could drive someday was sort of like promising the kids a puppy if the Cardinals won the Super Bowl—it just didn't seem like something we had to worry about. Brenda and I figured Zack would grow out of that phase before we had to deliver on it. But he never did.

Early on, just to appease him, we'd let him sit in our laps in the driveway and hold the wheel. But in St. Louis, a new opportunity arose. All of a sudden, we could afford what we wanted. We bought a house on a five-acre lot with woods and trails. We also bought a John Deere tractor. Brenda's dad had built John Deere tractors, but he could never afford one. Now we had one that we would use to drive around on the trails. Zack sat in my lap, and I'd drive all over our acreage. I don't think we ever used the tractor to mow the lawn; we just drove it for fun. And Brenda was okay with that because Zack was always in my lap.

Zack would have lived on that tractor if I had let him. Every day when I came home from work, I'd hear, "Dad, take me for a ride. Take me for a ride, please?"

I would take him for a ride, but no matter how long we went, it was never enough for Zack. And there were days I just didn't have the time. Finally one day, I said, "Zack, jump up on it by yourself and just be careful. We'll see if you can drive it alone."

So Zack started driving the tractor around in our circular driveway. I'd walk right next to him, watching to see how well he did. And though Brenda was anxious, she was fine with that arrangement because I was right there.

The next day, I let Zack drive the tractor without my standing next to him, as long as he went in one big circle so I could keep an eye on him. I'd go do something and then come back and check on him, but I always kept him in sight. That's when Brenda stopped being fine with it. It scared her, and she thought it was a bad idea. But the thing about Zack was that he was cautious; he never went crazy. Due to his visual impairment, he never likes to be in a situation where he feels out of control, so he took it very slow on the tractor.

But he did it by himself. And he loved it. He stayed on until he ran out of gas. As time went on, I got more comfortable, until Zack got to the point where he was able to take the tractor out by himself, even on the trails. He'd get it stuck sometimes, and I'd have to go out and help him, but that didn't stop him. Every day, he would drive that tractor for about two hours until it ran out of gas. When it quit, he'd come back and tell me the tractor was down by the creek or on the back trail, and I'd go pull it out. But the driving part he did all by himself.

Like I said, Brenda was scared at first. She'd always been Zack's protector, and now I was throwing caution to the wind—or throwing Zack to the tractor. But as she watched him stretch himself, and as he got better, he earned her confidence. In the process, we all learned more about what Zack is capable of doing.

I'm sure the fact that we let a blind boy drive a tractor all by himself wouldn't earn us any parenting awards. But it's what worked for us. Zack was able to get on the tractor in the first place because I wanted our kids to explore their interests even when it wasn't always safe for them to do so. But Zack was never injured. Probably because Brenda forced me to make sure Zack didn't try too much too quickly. Together, our parenting differences produced the best outcome for our son.

{ BRENDA }

Kurt and I aren't always in agreement. Sometimes I parent the same child differently from the way he does. For example, when Jesse started high school, she had a little more freedom and independence than she'd had before, but I still had rules for her to follow. When she wanted to spend the night at a friend's house, I called the parents to make sure they planned to be home. I also called to check on her during the night and to make sure she was where she was supposed to be.

Jesse hated this, and Kurt didn't think I should do it either. But I believe it set the foundation of expectations for her. Because she knew I was going to check up on her, she knew she had to be where she said she was going to be. I was able to gradually give her more responsibility and trust her each step of the way rather than wait until she screwed up and then take her freedom away. Because, let's face it, if I had waited until she screwed up, it could have been life-altering for her or for someone else. Because I set the standards right from the start, I believe Jesse and all my children were able to learn early on what was expected of them and how they could earn our trust.

Not only do Kurt and I parent the same child differently between us, but we also parent each child differently from his or her siblings. For instance, I made Jesse wait a long time before I let her wear makeup, but I started letting Jada wear it for her cheerleading competitions when she was eight. She doesn't get to wear it to school, only for performances when she's on stage. Jada already gets a lot of attention because she's cute—and she knows it. And she likes to be attractive. Instead of reinforcing that, I try to tell her how smart she is or how the clothes she chooses show her creativity.

On the other hand, I know that Jesse, like any seventeen-year-old, has a lot of doubts about her appearance, so I often tell her how beautiful she is. The girls could argue that I am not fair with them, but so what? There are lots of ways that I'm not fair. At night when I tuck Sierra into bed, I whisper in her ear, "You are my favorite." What she doesn't know is that I tell each of her siblings the same thing, most of them several times a day. Experts might say that is bad parenting. So what? It's just my little thing to do with them. Someday I hope they'll be sitting around talking and one of the kids will say, "Mom always told me I was her favorite." Then they'll learn the truth when the other six say, "She told me the same thing!"

Though my kids have certain rules they have to follow, *my* rule is that *I* have to adjust my parenting to each child's unique needs. I really believe that each child is uniquely and incredibly made by God.

Because he made me the parent of a creative child like Jesse, I've needed to learn how to parent a creative child. That has meant having plenty of art supplies on hand so that Jesse could use them when she was inspired to create. She and I have also talked a lot about creative things—like what she sees in a photograph or in the colors of nature.

Because God also made me the parent of a competitive child like Kade, I've needed to learn how best to parent a competitive child. For example, when I need Kade to run upstairs and get something, I tell him that I'll time him to see how long it takes. That would never work with Jesse; she'd move at the same pace no matter what. But it works with Kade because he wants to see how fast he can do it.

Though Jesse wouldn't have a problem making an abstract drawing, I sometimes ask Kade to create something abstract. He hates to do it, but it forces him to get outside his "have to be the best" mind-set.

Twenty years from now, the kids can tell us how they think we did, but until then, as we said in the last chapter, we just have to try our best.

Independence

One of the best things I've done with my kids is to make them as independent as they can be at each stage of their development. Whether it's getting themselves dressed and putting on their own shoes or setting their alarm clocks and making their own breakfasts, I've done everything I can to encourage their self-sufficiency. Each child is expected to be independent up to his or her ability. It's a survival thing; otherwise, Kurt and I are outnumbered.

It's interesting to compare our routine, with seven kids, to the routines of other parents with only one or two kids. Occasionally I'll call a girlfriend, and she'll say something like, "Can I call you back in twenty minutes? I'm putting Suzy down for bed, and she needs me to read to her, rock her, rub her back, and sing a special song to her before she'll go to sleep." Then, before she hangs up, she'll complain about doing that whole routine. But I'm thinking, *You've trained her to need this.*

I've learned that we teach people how to treat us. So if little Suzy really needs twenty minutes of hands-on personalized attention just to take a nap, it's because she's been taught to need it. And it's fine if that's what Suzy's mom wants to do, but then she shouldn't complain that it exhausts her or that she doesn't have enough time. She did it to herself.

Life is simpler when the kids are independent. For us, it's a necessity. When it's time to go somewhere, I need for the kids to put on their own shoes. As soon as my kids are old enough, I tell them, "You have to do this. I'm not going to put your shoes on for you." If I did it for everyone each time we left the house, we'd never get anywhere. The Babygirls are only three years old, so they can't tie yet, but they are capable of putting on their own mismatched pair of slip-on shoes. For the older ones, it means they learn to tie their own shoes. And brush their teeth.

Since middle school, Jesse has been setting her own alarm clock and getting herself up and ready. Maybe she'd like it if I made scrambled eggs and bacon every morning, but I hope she'll have other warm memories instead. At our house it's, "Everybody get your own bowl and milk. Get your own doughnuts."

My kids have learned to do their own homework each

night. No one looks over their shoulders to make sure they get it done. If they need help, it's their responsibility to ask for it. That's a big responsibility, but it makes them better communicators if they know that the only way to get help is to request it.

We teach our kids independence in much the same way that Kurt taught Zack how to drive the tractor. We put them into new situations and see how they do, while we stand to the side and monitor their progress. We're like the adult eagle that pushes the baby eagles out of the nest and watches to see if they can fly. If the fledglings start to fall, we're there to swoop down and grab them, and we'll keep trying until they get it right.

That kind of independence from such a young age gives the kids more opportunities to express their individuality. For instance, they get to show their own creativity each time they pick out their clothes. Are there days when they don't choose what I would have chosen? Sure. But if they dressed themselves and I didn't have to spend my time doing it, there's nothing wrong with that!

Some mothers think it's important that every little thing match. They put their child into a frilly little outfit with socks and shoes and a matching bow. Who cares? Does anyone really think that child dressed herself? No. One look at the child, and you know it's all about the mom.

Other moms have those huge, overstocked diaper bags. They're prepared for any emergency—spilled food, leaky diapers, or nuclear fallout. They even have a backup outfit for their child's backup outfit. That's not how I do it. We have a

bag that looks like a bag, and we toss a water bottle, hand san-
itizer, wet wipes, and maybe a few Band-Aids into it. If there's
an emergency, we just adapt to it. That's how we survive—by
teaching our kids to do it themselves, take care of themselves,
and solve their own problems. We're not going to spend the
rest of our lives looking over their shoulders to see what problems we can prevent. The best way to prepare kids for life is to
start training them to deal with life's problems now.

At the same time, I have to respect our children's individual needs. Not every child can be as independent as his or her
siblings were at that age. Take Zack, for example. Although
he had great moments of independence while driving the
tractor in St. Louis, when it comes to shower time, he needs
a lot of help. To learn to shower independently, he has to fight
against something that he can't control, and he hasn't gotten
there yet.

One of us has to stand at the door when he showers and
say, "Wet your hair." Then, "Here's the shampoo," and put it
in his hand. If I left him alone at that point, I'd come back
twenty minutes later, and he would still be standing there
because no one had given him any further instruction.

On the other hand, if Kade gets out of the shower and I
say, "Did you wash your hair?" and he tells me he didn't, I'll
make him go back in and wash it. We expect that level of
independence from Kade, but we don't from Zack.

Though I am all about protecting my kids, even keeping
them in a bubble sometimes, my goal is to guide them to
become independent and functioning adults. Our goal is

to nurture them until they're ready and then push them out of the nest so they can soar.

I want each of my kids to make mistakes, learn from them, and leave the nest ready for the life to which God has called him or her. Even Zack.

Our goal is for him to have a job someday. Based on what he likes right now, we think it might have something to do with trash—like picking up trash at a movie theater. But at the same time, as we teach him to be independent, we want to celebrate who he is and what he brings to our lives and to the lives of those he touches.

Recently, when Kurt's parents were in town for a visit, they asked Zack what he wanted to do.

"Ride the bus," he said.

Zack's been learning to use public transportation, because someday that's what he'll have to rely on. He rides the bus so often that when he took Grandpa and Grandma along for one of his rides, they were impressed to see that the driver knew him. He greeted Zack and turned the radio to Zack's favorite station. This is a guy who doesn't know that Zack is Kurt Warner's son. He laughed with Zack, and Kurt's parents had a great time talking with him.

Another man on the bus watched the interaction. When it came time for his stop, he stood, turned to Grandpa, and said, "I was having such a bad morning until I saw that young man with you. The smile on his face just made my day."

By the time Zack and his grandparents returned to the house, Grandpa had tears running down his face. Seeing Zack grow in his independence, and seeing him brighten other people's lives, made Grandpa happy.

Maybe because I have a special-needs child, I'm more likely to see the special needs in *each* of my children and try to respond to them as a parent. Like a good teacher, I want to train them in a way that will help them remember all that they've learned. But I won't know for another twenty years how I've done. In the meantime, I have to trust God that I'm making the right choices for each of them. The hard part of that is developing trust, because to truly trust, I have to let go, even when I'm not ready.

CHAPTER 7

blessings and burdens come together

{ KURT }

My career has provided the highest of highs—a Super Bowl win—and the lowest of lows—being benched or, worse, let go from a team. But that's life. And that's something I've tried to teach my kids. Everyone's life will have its ups and downs, and there's no reason to spend much time focusing on one or the other.

Playing in a Super Bowl has some nice perks—trips to nice places, invitations to cool parties, and dinners with celebrities. Because of my job, I get to meet people I never could have imagined meeting while I was growing up in Iowa—like the president of the United States.

After the Super Bowl in Tampa, we flew back to Phoenix. I was driving home from the airport when a private call came through on my caller ID. Usually, I don't answer those, but for whatever reason, I answered this one.

The person on the line said, "Mr. Warner?" That's always a giveaway that it isn't someone I know, so I never say yes. I said what I always say: "Who's this?"

"Mr. Warner?" he asked again.

"Who's this?" I repeated.

Finally, the guy on the phone introduced himself. I don't remember his name, but he said, "I've got the president here. He'd like to talk to you, if you've got a minute."

The president of the United States is asking if I've got a minute?

So President Obama came on the line and said that he's a big fan, that he appreciated what I had done this year, and that it was a great Super Bowl. Then he said he really enjoyed watching me on the football field, probably because I'm the one closest to his age. So he even cracked an "old" joke on me. I told him I was looking forward to watching his presidency and that I would be praying for him. It was short and sweet, but it was cool.

When I got home and told the kids, each had a different reaction. Kade kept saying, "Get out of here!" but Jesse wanted to know what he'd said. The Babygirls just wanted dinner.

That wasn't the first time I'd spoken to a president. Once, I was invited to speak at the Pentagon, and afterward Brenda and I were invited to the White House. There, we sat in a room with about twelve other people, most of whom were also speakers from the event. As President Bush made his way around the room to greet everyone, one of his assistants would introduce each person to the president.

When he got to me, the president said, "Hey, Kurt, how are you doing? I'm a big fan."

That was pretty cool. I mean, how often do you meet the

president of the United States and no one has to introduce you because he knows who you are?

But here's the funny part: What Brenda remembers most wasn't the fact that the leader of the free world was a fan of her husband. It wasn't even the impressive White House decor. What Brenda remembers most was that President Bush had hair coming out of his ears.

It drove her crazy.

"If you were the president, wouldn't you say, 'Somebody needs to be in charge of trimming my ear hair'?" She couldn't stop talking about it afterward. She thought it should be someone's job to keep it trimmed and that this person had failed miserably.

Meeting the president was certainly a high for me, but as often happens, Brenda brought me back to earth when she reminded me that I was only a few ear hairs away from being the butt of someone's joke. And though it may not be a rule, it's always a good reminder that no matter what our job is, we're all still human.

Hidden Blessings

In our backyard, we have a trampoline. It's sunk into the ground, so we don't have to have all that extra netting, and it's safe for even the youngest children. Our kids love to bounce on it. They'll jump as high as they can, and while they're in the air, they'll twist and turn so you never know which body part will hit the trampoline and bounce them up again. Occasionally, they miss and hit the ground, but when they do, they pick themselves up and start jumping again.

We also have a balance beam in our backyard. It's not very high, just a few inches off the ground, but it challenges the kids' coordination. Lean too far to the left or to the right, and they'll fall off. But if they stare straight ahead and just keep going, they'll almost always make it to the end.

Both pieces of equipment symbolize what I want for my kids' lives. I want them to have new and exciting experiences—like our trampoline offers. I want them to leap into the sky with little regard for what's below them. To go as high as they can and know that even if they miss, they can try again. And along the way, I hope they experience the twists and turns of all kinds of new highs. I also want them to live life as if it were a balance beam—concentrating on the end goal and not always looking side to side. They're more likely to get derailed from their goals if they don't focus on the end prize. My life has brought highs, lows, moments of focus, and moments when I got derailed, but each experience has taught me something about myself.

In football, the worst moments I've had really stunk. But I picked myself up and continued to press toward the goal, whatever it was at the time. Along the way, I learned another rule that we try to teach our kids: Sometimes there are hidden blessings when things don't work out the way we planned.

A few years ago, when Brenda was pregnant with the twins, she was confined to bed rest. But when things took a turn for the worse, her doctor admitted her to the hospital. The kids were scared and confused; they thought Mom wasn't ever coming home. There were also concerns about the babies' health. In addition, our babysitter had just quit, and we hadn't yet hired a nanny, so we were trying to do it all alone.

Brenda was hospitalized right before the second-to-last game of the season. That Sunday, she was watching the game from her hospital bed when she heard, "Warner's down." Nothing scares a quarterback's wife more than those words. As she lay in bed, they kept replaying the hit that had taken me out. Over and over again. In slow motion. I'm sure it looked horrible (I know it *felt* horrible), but there was nothing Brenda could do. She couldn't even sit up.

On the field, I knew the injury was bad enough to keep me out for the final game. But I also knew I'd be okay, and I'd be able to make it home that night. I asked to borrow a cell phone, and from the sideline I called Brenda's room to reassure her. "I'm fine. It's just my knee. No big deal. I'll be home tonight. You just take care of yourself and those baby girls." I didn't want her to go into early labor.

The next morning, Brenda had a C-section. Sierra and Sienna were born healthy, at five pounds each. That's when we discovered the hidden blessing from my injury—I didn't have to go in to work the next day. I was done for the season and could stay home with Brenda and the new babies.

Sometimes my kids, especially Kade, will get so mad about losing a game that they can't focus on anything else. At those moments, I try to teach them that good can still come out of a loss. Maybe they learned some new skills, or they learned not to give up when the odds were against them.

But I know how they feel. It's much easier to stay in that bad place—mad and angry at the world and questioning what you could have done differently—than it is to pick yourself up and keep moving.

One of my lowest times took place when the twins were about a year old. It was Veterans Day, and Brenda was jumping on the trampoline with Elijah when all of a sudden her back hurt like it had never hurt before. I was at work, so she had to crawl upstairs to her room by herself while Elijah ran for help. The pain was so bad that she was eventually forced to go to the emergency room, where they did an X-ray and discovered a ruptured disk. Surgery was required immediately, and the doctor was concerned that Brenda might incur paralysis in one of her legs.

On top of all that, I had just been benched from my starting-quarterback position. It looked like my career was over, and I was frustrated because I knew I had more in me, but I might not be given the opportunity to prove it. I got Brenda's call while I was at practice and immediately left for the hospital, arriving just before they put her under anesthesia.

Fortunately, the surgery went fine, and a few days later, she was able to come home. One of her friends, Stacy, who has a nursing degree, came to help us, but I was still overwhelmed with trying to work and take care of the kids. It would have been easy to allow the unfairness of the situation to distract me. But I stayed engaged—focused on what I was doing at both work and at home—and kept my eye on the end goals—getting Brenda healthy and earning back my starting position. And because I did, there was a huge payoff.

Three days after Brenda came home from her back surgery,

she got a cramp in her leg. Neither she nor Stacy thought much about it. But something really bothered me about it. I insisted we call the doctor and then took Brenda in to see him. After an examination, he discovered a blood clot in her leg that could have killed her within seconds. She didn't have any of the traditional symptoms—it wasn't red, swollen, or hot to the touch—so although both Brenda and Stacy were nurses, they'd missed it.

Brenda required another emergency surgery so they could put in a filter to catch the clot before it got to her heart and killed her. For the next six months, she was on blood thinners.

I don't know much about medical stuff, but I do know that I had felt a strong compulsion to have my wife looked at immediately. I listened to that prompting even though it would've been easy to ignore it or to listen to Brenda and Stacy, who thought it was just a cramp. After all, they were the medical experts. But I was focused on taking care of Brenda.

During that time, a lot of football experts were saying I was done. I didn't listen to them, either. I continued to work as hard on the field as I did off the field. Despite what everyone said, I believed I could earn back the starting-quarterback position.

And I did.

Two years later, I took my team to the Super Bowl.

That's also what we teach our kids. Regardless of the setbacks you face and the opposition in front of you, you have to be able to pick yourself up and try again.

{ BRENDA }

Kurt mentioned hidden blessings, but with every blessing can also come a burden. Kurt's job is a huge blessing to us as a family, but occasionally the kids have to shoulder burdens that they might not otherwise face.

Once, a fan asked Kurt to sign some things for him as he left the practice facility with Jada. This particular fan was waiting outside, and Kurt had signed a lot of stuff for him in the past, so he didn't feel bad about saying, "Not this time, man. I'm with my kid."

But then the guy followed them in his car. It scared Jada.

Kurt finally pulled over and talked to the guy, telling him that he just couldn't do stuff like that.

The threat may not have been significant, but Jada's fear was.

I understand her concerns. It's happened to me, too. A couple of weeks after Super Bowl XLIII, some friends had just left the house, and the nanny and I were alone with the girls. Four guys walked up to the gate and pushed the button. "Is Kurt Warner home?" they asked when I answered the buzzer.

"What do you need?" I asked.

"Well, we're here on vacation to see the Diamondbacks. We're baseball fans, not football fans, but someone said Kurt Warner lived here, so we were just wondering if he's home."

Seriously? I mean, that's the best you've got? "We're baseball fans"?

The guys eventually left, but you never know about people in those situations. Unfortunately, as many celebrities can testify, curious fans don't look much different from potentially dangerous ones.

I understand that football is a big deal to a lot of people.

But my kids aren't interested in football, so it's not a topic they talk about much. Yet sometimes when the team isn't doing well or Kurt's had a bad game, the bus driver or kids at school will discuss it with my kids—as if my kids choose plays with their dad over the dinner table. Sometimes they're put in a position where they feel as if they have to defend their dad, and they're not even sure why.

Jesse said once, "I wonder how they'd like it if I went up to them and told them their dad did really bad at his last business meeting."

That's one of the burdens of being a Warner kid; you never get to be completely normal. Last week, Jesse was at a musical festival. She already felt intimidated because she wasn't sure if she was good enough to be there. Once the person in charge found out who she was, she started getting special attention—but not for her musical talents. I'll let her tell you what happened:

> *The lady that was running the entire regional choir found out who my dad is and bugged me to get her an autograph. Here I am, scared to death, just humbled to be around all these people who are so much better than I am at something I love to do, and then she's like, "So, do I get an autograph?"*
>
> *It's just not what I want to be dealing with, ever.*

So when the kids complain that it's not fair or that they don't deserve it, we remind them of the rule. And this isn't just a Warner rule; it's a life rule: If you want the blessing, you have to take the burdens that go along with it.

And, of course, they always want the blessing.

One of the greatest blessings of Kurt's job is that we get to travel and take the kids with us. When Jesse and Zack were little, the only big buildings they ever saw were the ones in Des Moines. The year that Kurt got into the Arena Bowl, it was in Phoenix, I think, and the kids went with us. I remember the first time they saw the buildings of downtown Phoenix. They were so excited. They started pointing and yelling, "Look at the Des Moines buildings!"

Now we have a house in Cabo San Lucas, Mexico, and we take the kids there several times a year. No one knows who we are, and our kids have a lot of freedom to just run and play. But the really cool part is that they get to experience a totally different culture—a different language, different foods, and kids who look different but who love to play the same games. My kids often play with the local children, and though they don't speak the same language, they always find ways to communicate.

So that's our job as parents—to even out the highs and lows and teach our children how to balance the blessings and the burdens. One of the best ways to do that is to spend time alone with each child. With seven kids, it's often hard to find time for each kid to have private one-on-one time with Kurt and me. But that's been another blessing of his job. Each season, Kurt plays half his games in other cities. We've started taking the kids along to these games, not only to let them see and experience new things but also to get some uninterrupted one-on-one time with them.

At the beginning of every season, I get out my big

calendar, and we sit down as a family and look at the schedule. Everybody gets to look at the cities and pick which one they'd like to go to. The rule is, if they've already been to that city, they can't go again—we want them to experience new places. If a specific game falls around the time of their birthday, we encourage them to pick that game. Then it becomes an extra-special birthday weekend, because they'll get a few extra gifts. Other times they pick a city—like Jada picked Chicago one year—because it's close to grandparents and other family. The kids all have their own reasons for their choices.

During those weekends away, the kids get to decide when and where they want to eat. They never get to do that at home. I'll ask, "What would you choose to eat if you could pick anything?" If it's ten in the morning and Zack says he wants to have hot wings, I have to find a place that has hot wings at ten in the morning. If I have to, I'll even beg the hotel chef to make them, because how often do you get to choose what you want to eat when you're in a family of nine?

There are very few rules during those weekends. The younger kids just want to stay in and have room service, relax, and watch movies. They'll drink chocolate shakes for breakfast and pick the same meal three times in a row. For one of them, it was chicken and a Coke. Always chicken and a Coke.

I want each child to feel like he or she is special, so I'll often arrange to have a little gift waiting on the bed when we arrive. For Zack, it might be new headphones; for Jada, it might be an American Girl doll outfit. It's just a way of showing them I recognize their special interests.

An hour at an art museum is mandatory on each trip. Not only do we go there to instill an appreciation of art, but I'm also trying to get my kids to pay attention to details, look at things in new ways, and talk about what they see.

For example, when Jada was six, we went to San Francisco. We visited a museum with beautiful sculptures attached to the outside of the building. We sat outside, and while she drank a soda and I had coffee, I asked her to point out the shapes she recognized in the sculptures. She found circles, squares, and triangles. Then we talked about what she felt as she looked at the art. I wanted her to use her words to communicate what she was seeing and thinking about.

As parents, unless we make one-on-one time with our kids a priority, we don't have the time to say, "Tell me what you see." But when we do, their answers are a great way to learn a lot about what they're thinking.

I am very deliberate about the conversation in those moments. I ask them who they want to be when they grow up. I ask them about their friends at school and who they think will still be their friend ten years from now.

Kurt flies on the team plane, and he usually joins us for dinner on Saturday night. As much as possible, I try to get a private table, or we get room service, just so the child can have Daddy by him- or herself for an hour.

So, although I sometimes complain that Kurt's celebrity takes him away from the kids or means there are interruptions during family dinners, I also recognize there are some incredible blessings.

But the kids aren't the only ones who have to learn the

balance between the blessings and the burdens. Since Kurt's first season in the NFL, I am no longer known as Brenda. Now I am known as "Kurt Warner's wife." That was hard for a woman as independent as I am. But the upside is that, as Kurt's wife, more people want to hear what I have to say.

For example, about ten years ago there was a women's expo in St. Louis. Mia Farrow was scheduled to speak, but she canceled at the last minute, and I was asked to fill in. I was offered that speaking engagement because I was Kurt's wife. And because it was so last minute, I got paid the same amount they were going to pay Mia Farrow—$10,000.

Along with that check, I also took home a few expectations. Not long after we moved to Phoenix, I heard that the same group was having an event here. They arranged for me to speak at that event also, but I was told they couldn't afford to pay me. I agreed anyway. People said it would be a great event, and it would be my "coming out" to the community—something that would ultimately get me other speaking engagements. That sounded good to me.

It was a big event—held at the football stadium—so I asked seven people to come with me: a couple of girlfriends, my friend Lorena (whom I am teaching English), and Jesse. When we arrived at the stadium, I went to check in and no one knew who I was or why I was there. After a couple of conversations through their headsets, they figured it out and guided me and my girls to the inside of the stadium.

I immediately saw that the entire field was covered with booths—people who wanted to sell products and services. Instead of a main stage in the center of the stadium, as I had expected, there was a small wooden platform built at the front of one section. In other words, I would not be speaking to a stadium full of people; I would be speaking to section 121.

At the time, the actress Gabrielle Union was on the stage. She's beautiful, and she was doing a great job. The audience was laughing, and I could see they loved her. But as I looked at the audience from the back, I realized that all I could see was dark hair. As I got a little closer, I realized why—her entire audience was black.

My first thought was, *Okay, this is something new. I hope they're interested in what I have to say.*

Gabrielle finished her talk and headed up the stairs to the mezzanine level to do a signing. I started down the stairs so I could get to the stage where I was supposed to speak. But as my seven white friends and I tried to work our way down, we were faced with a sea of black faces coming up the stairs to go to Gabrielle's signing. By the time I got to the stage, there was no one left in the audience.

Someone took me "backstage" until it was my time to go on. Backstage wasn't the plush green room that Kurt usually gets; no, for me it was a step. So I sat on the step and waited for my cue.

As I was waiting, I heard Tara, a local television personality, introducing me. But as I listened, I realized her facts were wrong. She was using a version of the e-mail that Kurt mentioned in chapter 1, and none of it was true. Everything I was about to say would contradict what she had just told the audience.

I was so busy rewriting my speech in my head that I almost

missed my cue. But as I walked onstage, I could see that I didn't need to worry. There were only seven people sitting in the stands—the six friends I had brought with me, and Jesse.

Actually, there was one more: a guy sitting front and center—at the women's expo—wearing a #13 Warner jersey.

I found my spot in the center of the stage, but it was also the center of a pile of hair. Apparently, they had done make-overs on the stage in an earlier session and no one had bothered to sweep it up.

Like an idiot, I just went on with what I had planned as my intro: "How many of you have ever been on food stamps?"

One hand went up. Jesse's.

"How many of you here have lost somebody that you love?"

Again one hand went up; again, it was Jesse's. She was beaming like she was the proudest daughter in the world, and all I could think was, *These seven people already know my story, and I'm not getting paid, so why even bother?*

But I continued. By now, a few people who had gotten their Gabrielle Union autographs had trickled back in. But it was only a trickle. So, on the fly, I cut out the entire middle section of my speech and got off the stage as fast as I could, kicking the tufts of hair out of my new sandals as I went. But then I realized there was nowhere to go. There was no back-stage, other than that little step, and by now there was probably another speaker already sitting on it. So I started back up the stairs to the mezzanine where I'd come from.

As I climbed the steps, I noticed a man heading toward me. He had a grin on his face and a card in his hand.

"Great job," he said. "Here's my card. I'd love to get Kurt to come speak at my event."

Kurt?

Behind him, a woman from the audience held out her hand. I shook it and said, "Thanks for coming." She didn't say anything.

Another man behind her was holding out his hand, so I grabbed it and said, "Thank you, thank you so much for coming."

And he said, "I'm the audio guy; give me your microphone."

That's how far I'd come—from $10,000 to "give me your microphone."

I've learned, though, that over time things always have a way of evening out. I received an invitation to speak at the expo again this coming year. This time, they'll pay me $1,500, and I'll be on the main stage, with my name on the Jumbo-Tron. And Tara, the woman who introduced me? Well, she has become a close friend, and we laugh about how I'll be sure to have someone else introduce me this year.

If I had gotten bent out of shape because that last engagement wasn't very good, if I had left angry and pouting instead of laughing, I would have missed out on the blessings that followed.

I guess that's what I want my kids to know: In the end, everything works out for good, even if it's not what you originally planned. There are blessings and burdens to being the wife or kids of Kurt Warner. Sometimes they're directly related to what's happening to him on the field; often they're not. But there are blessings and burdens in everyone's life. And though our lives are richer because of the highs and lows we've had, we want our kids to focus on their own goals and not to be distracted by all the other stuff. We want them to find their own sense of joy and worth amid life's ups and downs.

After that expo experience, I asked my friend Lorena what she thought. "You are a very good speaker, Brenda, but I do not speak English so good to understand what you say."

At least she called me Brenda.

CHAPTER 8

treat others better than yourself

(even if they play for the Steelers)

{ KURT }

As I mentioned before, Zack is fascinated with radios, and he loves music. So when we learned that his favorite group, the Black Eyed Peas, would be performing before the opening game of the 2006 season, we wanted to take Zack. Even though he hates football games (because of the loud fireworks), he agreed to go if he could hear his number one group.

As a special treat, Brenda talked to the PR guy and arranged a meet and greet with the Black Eyed Peas during halftime. At the appointed time, Brenda and Zack went to the suite. The band members were watching the game with some of their friends, and everyone seemed to be having a good time. Brenda entered the suite and Zack followed, using his cane. Seeing that Zack was blind, the band members rose to greet him. One at a time, they put out their hands and introduced themselves.

"Thank you so much for being a fan," one of the musicians said to Zack.

"It's awesome you like our music," said another.

At that point, Zack was getting nervous, so he pulled his sleeves down over his hands and started scratching his eyebrows. The more nervous he gets, the more he scratches.

Now remember, Zack's sense of hearing is very well developed. So when he heard a female voice say, "Hey, who's this?" he knew it was Fergie. He got even more nervous and started scratching even harder.

"Hi, I'm Brenda Warner and this is Zack, Kurt Warner's son. He's a big fan, and he'd love to meet you."

"Hey, Zack," she said.

Before she could say anything else, Zack said, "You stink."

"What?"

"You stink," Zack repeated as he started to sway while still scratching his forehead.

Of course at that point, Brenda wanted to die. So she tried to explain.

"What he means is that you smell really good. Because he has such a strong sense of smell . . . uh, that's just his way of saying that he likes the way you smell."

Brenda was trying anything because she was so embarrassed. "So, he's blind and he thinks you smell good."

"Well, thank you, Zack," Fergie said, and then she posed for a picture with him.

Fergie has probably forgotten all about it by now, but Brenda hasn't. She was mortified for days. One of the rules we teach our kids is that it's important to treat others better than we treat ourselves. Zack's words to Fergie weren't exactly what we had in mind.

We want our kids to put others first, to not notice their differences, and to love them like Jesus would. When that doesn't happen, it gets our attention more than some of the other rules.

At Restaurants

My wife is really creative in coming up with fun ways to teach the kids how we want them to treat others. You've already read about a couple of these from the *New York Times* article, but let me try to flesh them out a bit.

When we would take the kids to a restaurant, the hostess usually gave the younger ones crayons and a coloring sheet to keep them busy until the food came. That was fine, but what typically happened next wasn't. When the server asked for our order, the kids would either mumble what they wanted or yell it in the server's direction without looking up.

We don't want our kids to do that. We want them to look other people in the eye, talk to them politely, and treat them with respect. Brenda and I have both worked jobs where people didn't look us in the eye. Even after I won the Super Bowl, there were many times when Brenda would be standing right next to me and someone would come up and never even acknowledge that she was there. I don't think those people tried to be rude; I just think they weren't taught what to do in a situation like that—to acknowledge both parties and look directly at them.

The easy way for us to teach our children is to tell them—reminding them again and again—to look the server in the eye. But after a while, even the most attentive child will tune us out. And some of our kids are still too young to under-stand what we're trying to do. Those who are old enough to understand don't want to be preached at. So that's why Brenda came up with some creative ways to teach our kids respect for others.

For example, rule #4 from the *New York Times* article: After we've placed our order and the server has left the table, the kids have to tell Brenda what color the server's eyes were. The only way they'll know is if they look the person in the eye when they're placing their orders. It's a simple rule and can be fun for the kids, but it also helps them to be respectful to the people they come in contact with.

Eating out provides other opportunities to teach our kids how to treat others. After my first season in St. Louis, my face was all over the media, and people started recognizing me. Whenever we'd go out for dinner, people were always picking up the check. The manager would come over and say, "Don't worry about it. It's on the house." For the first time in our lives, Brenda and I could afford to eat what we wanted, wher-ever we wanted, and yet now someone else was always paying the bill. That's when we first realized that the old saying "the rich get richer" really was true.

When Brenda was a single mom, she couldn't afford to take her kids out to eat very often. When she did, she wouldn't order an appetizer or dessert, and she'd drink water so that Zachary and Jesse could get what they wanted. It would have been such a blessing back then if someone had picked up her tab.

After I started earning good money in the NFL, we decided

to bless other families by paying for their meals. (That's where rule #1 from the article came from.) Now when we go out to eat, the kids look around the restaurant and then all agree on a family. Once they've agreed, we tell our server that we want to pay that family's bill. Doing that offers many lessons for our kids about sharing our blessings, considering those less fortunate, and knowing that even little things can make a difference. Now that the kids are getting older, Brenda and I are happy to see that they're understanding all that. Here's what Jesse recently said:

> *I think Mom and Dad are always trying to remind us that we are really blessed. It's their way of reminding us of the big picture and helping us to realize what our purpose is, why we're here, and really what our duty is when we've been given all these blessings. I think it's important, especially with the younger ones, just for them to know that you can make a difference. That's what you're supposed to do. And you're supposed to use all these worldly treasures so that you can help the people around you.*

For a parent, there is nothing better than seeing your kids get the things you are trying to teach them.

There are other, more subtle, lessons that we try to teach through that same family activity. The kids learn how to make decisions together and come to an agreement. They learn to listen to their brothers and sisters and to value each person's opinion. We could preach those things, but when we put our

kids in situations where they have to figure it out for themselves, they're much more likely to remember what we're trying to teach—and much more likely to transfer the lesson to
other situations.

In some ways, that little family tradition became the training wheels for the other things we ask our kids to do, such as
getting involved with our First Things First Foundation. But
what really works about that dinner-buying rule is that our
kids see "loving your neighbor" in action. It's not an arbitrary
discussion about sharing your blessings with others; they actually choose who to share them with.

We always ask the server not to tell the other family. It's
best when they don't find out, and it spares all of us some
awkward moments. But occasionally word gets to the family anyway, and they find out who paid. That happened in
Tampa while we were there for the Super Bowl.

Brenda and I were eating with friends at the Cheesecake
Factory, and we noticed another family. It was a large family, maybe twenty people, and you could just see that they
were all having a good time together and enjoying each other's
company. We told our server that we wanted to take care of
their bill and asked him not to tell the other family, but the
family still found out we'd paid for them. Next thing I knew,
a really big guy came up to me at our table.

"Thanks, man, for buying our meal. I really appreciate it,"
he said.

"No problem," I said, trying to make it short and sweet
and avoid any awkward conversation. But he kept talking.

"Just wanted to introduce myself," he said. "Even though

I won't be playing this weekend, I'm on the Pittsburgh Steelers roster."

After he left, we laughed about that—especially when Brenda pointed out that some of the people at the table were wearing black and gold. Though I would have liked to give that particular check back, we didn't do anything more than joke about it. And I hope how I handled it will teach our kids another lesson—maybe one about loving your enemies (or at least your opponents).

Sometimes we see these lessons pay off in other ways. Recently, while Kade was playing Pop Warner football, a player from the other team got hurt. Kade went over to the injured boy and laid his hands on him and prayed. When Kade got up, his coach was mad.

"What are you doing? Pray for him when you get home! You don't pray for him here. Huddle up!"

Moments like that make me proud, and they help me realize that the kids are picking up the lessons we're trying to teach.

We think that part of treating others better than ourselves is learning to pay attention to the little things—like stacking dishes at the end of the meal to make the server's job easier, or picking up our own trash at the end of a movie. They're small things, but things that we hope will make the kids understand there are ways they can serve others instead of always being the ones served.

Encouraging Others

I want my kids to encourage each other and those around them. That's one reason why I'm careful to model that

behavior for them. For example, when my kids are playing sports, I'm not one of those dads who is always yelling,
"Throw the ball!" or "Kick it!"

Even in football, where I have some credibility, I never give
advice to the coaches or the players. My rule is to only say
encouraging things, because that's what I want my kids to do.
Sometimes it's hard not to say something, because the coaches
don't know a lot about the game and they're not always teaching the right things. Like with Kade, they'll say, "Block that
guy!" But they don't tell him how; they just tell him to do it.

I want to go over and say, "These kids don't have a chance,
because they aren't being coached right." But I also don't want
to jump in, because the coaches are volunteering their time to
work with the kids and I'm not. Instead, I'll find ways of supporting and encouraging my child.

I always tell Kade, "I'd be happy to help you out," but he
never asks me for help. Never. And I'm fine with that. I don't
want to be the kind of dad who just *has* to involve himself.
So, at games, I'm always positive, and I just cheer for the kids.
At their ages, it shouldn't be about winning and losing anyway; it should be about having fun, and I just want to encourage them in that.

Brenda rolls her eyes at me because I'll cheer for the other
team, especially at Jada's softball games. When someone gets
a good hit for the other team, I'll yell, "Good hit, number
four," or whatever. When Jada bobbles a ball, I only notice
how hard she tried to get it. "Way to go, Jada!"

Even though my job as a quarterback is to win games,
when it comes to my kids, my job is to be their number one

encourager. And no matter how well, or how badly, they play, I hope they're the number one encourager on their teams as well.

{ BRENDA }

Our kids are very fortunate that they live such privileged lives, and we never want them to take that for granted. We always want them to be grateful for what they have yet never hold on to it so tightly that they can't share what they have with someone else. That's why one of our rules is to treat others better than they treat themselves. We try to teach this lesson in several ways, not only to remind the kids but to remind ourselves. For example, when Jesse walks into a room, we want her to think, *What can I do? How can I serve someone else?* And though she's gotten really good at serving others through the foundation, we want her to look for opportunities to serve in the small things at home.

Even though we have housekeepers who come in to clean, our kids have Saturday-morning chores and are expected to keep their own messes picked up. It's a respect issue. The housekeepers are there to clean, not to *clean up* after the kids. So the night before they come, I'll remind Jesse to pick up her stuff.

"Jesse, you need to clean up for the cleaning ladies."

"What? The *cleaning* lady? Why do I need to *clean* for the *cleaning* lady?"

"Because it's not her job to pick up that bowl of cereal you left on the couch last night. It's not her job."

The kids know that if they leave something lying around

long enough, someone else will eventually pick it up for them. So I've had to start telling the housekeepers, "Don't pick this up, because our kids need to do their part," or "Don't clean Jesse's room unless you can see the floor."

It's weird, I know, to pay someone to clean your house and then tell them not to do something. I am not saying we've got it all figured out; our kids could do so much more. But it's just one of the ways we try to teach our kids that they can't expect other people to clean up after them. Of course, this is a lesson I often need to learn myself. So sometimes when I'm telling the kids they need to pick up, I'm thinking, *So do I.*

Appearances

One of the other things we don't ever want our kids to do is to judge other people by their outward appearance. We want them to look at the heart. When we're at Disney World with the Make-A-Wish children, we want our kids to see a buddy, not a boy who is missing his lower jaw. When they see kids in wheelchairs or kids who have a tube coming out of their nose, we want them to look past the medical needs and see a new friend. We never want them to judge people by their appearance, and that includes the color of their skin.

Although that's something we constantly teach, there are always opportunities to make the lessons stick. For example, when Kurt and Larry Fitzgerald were on *The Tonight Show with Jay Leno*, Larry told Jay a story about what happened at the Pro Bowl.

Not only is Larry a great receiver for the Cardinals, but he's also one of Kurt's friends. Sometimes he hangs out at our house—he's building a new home near us—and he and Kurt often end up at the same events together. My kids all know him, and they like to hang out and joke around with him. Especially Elijah. Larry is Elijah's favorite football player, as you already know from the Toaster Strudel incident. To Elijah, anything Larry says goes. That's why Elijah wears his hair in a Mohawk. It was Larry who told him it looked good that way.

But the Babygirls don't like Larry. For some reason, they're scared to death of him.

So when Kurt and Larry were on Jay Leno, Larry started telling Jay a story about talking to Elijah when we were all in Hawaii for the Pro Bowl. Larry had asked Elijah, "Why don't your baby sisters like me?"

Then Larry told Jay (and millions of viewers) that Elijah said, "It's the color of your skin."

So, of course, Kurt had to explain to Jay what we actually teach our children. Larry, fortunately, already knew that, but it's one example of how we have to continually stay on guard, teaching our kids not to judge based on appearances.

Looking beyond appearances is one of the reasons we started CHEER—Consciousness Helps Encourage Equal Respect—a program for high schoolers. We take the program to high schools, and we select volunteers—often student leaders and athletes—to demonstrate what it's like to live with a disability. It's an eye-opening experience for the student body to see those students struggle with their new limitations.

First thing in the morning, the participants each put on a CHEER Leader T-shirt, and then they go to the gymnasium and pick a piece of paper out of a basket. On each piece of paper is written a disability. Whatever disability they pick, they have to live with for the day. There are no second chances or switching with a friend. Some of them will say, "Can I switch? Because that's my dominant hand." That makes me laugh—as if you get to pick where you have a disability.

We have a variety of ways to simulate different disabilities. For example, for someone who has "lost a limb," we sling them up so they can't use one of their arms or legs. We create "blindness" in different forms, using goggles that mimic peripheral-vision loss, cataracts, or complete blindness. The kids wear sound-reducing earphones to make them "deaf." Others are in wheelchairs and can't use their legs. The students immediately take on whatever disability they've been assigned, and they vow to live with it all day.

Then they go to class. That's when they must begin to adapt to their disability. They see how other people treat them—how nobody opens doors; how everyone rushes by them in the hall; how people don't leave enough space to get through. They see how other kids might intentionally or unintentionally trip them. If they're in a wheelchair, they see how people avoid looking at them and how they can't make eye contact with people standing around them.

Because the students now, for the first time, have special needs, they're late to every class, and they can't find time to go to the bathroom because it takes so much longer.

The demonstration is also educational for the students who aren't in the program. They get to see someone with great athletic ability struggle without the use of his right arm.

It levels the playing field. At the same time, I hope it makes them realize that kids with disabilities might have other abilities that we have a hard time seeing.

I would love for the kids to go home with their disabilities—to ride the bus, get around the house, and go to sleep with their limitations—but for liability reasons, we can't do that. Instead, at the end of the day, the students turn in their disabilities. When they come in the next morning, they pick another random disability—maybe it's the same one, or maybe it's different—and start learning how to adapt.

At the end of the week, Kurt and I lead an assembly for the whole school. The interest level of the students always pleases me. If you haven't been to a high school assembly lately, let me tell you that the students often aren't very well behaved. Many of them talk and don't listen, and when the principal gets up to speak, people boo him.

But at our last assembly, it was so quiet you could have heard a pin drop. I know some of that has to do with Kurt; he obviously gets a lot of attention. But they still listened intently when I got up to speak. I explained what it's like to be the mom of a child who has never been invited to a birthday party, a mom whose son will never drive a car or play sports. Zack can never text me or text his friends. I tell the students that he didn't choose that life, and he doesn't deserve it.

Then I tell them how many head injuries happen to high school students. I explain that any one of them could go from being healthy to being permanently disabled in one quick, unexpected event. The numbers are unbelievable.

"Count five people down," I'll tell them. "Most likely,

one of you is going be in an accident sometime during your lifetime."

I created CHEER because as the mother of a child with a disability, I love how many people the program reaches. Not only are the CHEER Leaders affected by the experience, but so are the kids who don't participate but watch the CHEER Leaders struggle. Each volunteer in the program has friends who have to help carry books or open doors, so it affects them, too.

The program also affects the teachers. When they have CHEER Leaders in their classes, the teachers have to take different and more creative approaches to teaching those children. They have to figure out a way to make sure the disabled student learns the lesson. It gets the teachers out of their own little boxes and helps them become better at their jobs.

My hope is that the kids will go home and talk about CHEER with their parents and that as a result of that experience, people will change their behavior in the smallest of ways—say, opening a door for someone who needs help—and in bigger ways, such as volunteering for a week at the Special Olympics.

I want the students not to look at appearances and not to associate kids with their disabilities. Instead of walking by and ignoring people with special needs—or worse, making fun of them—I want people to see behind the limp or the wheelchair to the real person.

Those are the same lessons we try to teach our kids each day—to look beyond appearances to see the real person. To see another person's heart—and to love them for who they are.

CHAPTER 9

share your blessings

{ KURT }

Waiting for the press conference to begin, looking at the cameras, the microphones, and the reporters wanting to capture my every word, I thought of how many times I had dreamed of this exact situation. It was hard to believe it was happening. Winning the Super Bowl helped me earn my first big contract with the Rams. It was for something like $46 million. After I signed the agreement, the media gathered to ask a few questions. They asked about the team, the negotiations, and then about the contract.

At that point in my career, most of the members of the press knew I was a Christian and what I stood for. A few questions about my faith came up. Then, from the back of the room, a reporter asked, "Kurt, are you going to tithe from all $46 million in your contract?"

It was the first time I'd thought about that.

I had been tithing since my Arena Football days. Once I became a believer, it was one of those things I never wavered in. The Bible said to do it, so as far as I was concerned, I was locked in. But now I faced writing a check with more zeros in it than the lottery jackpot. That money could buy houses, college educations, and so much more.

Without hesitation, I told the reporter yes, I was going to tithe from all $46 million.

And I did.

Brenda and I tithe 10 percent of everything we make. That's our rule. Always. But it isn't always easy to write the check. Whether my income is high—like it is now—or low, as it was in the early days of Arena Football, there are many reasons *not* to give our money away. No matter how large the check, some days it's still hard to hand it over.

Growing up in a house with a single mom, I never had a lot of money. That taught me not to depend on it; as easy as it comes, it can also go. But when almost overnight you get a large amount, it can have the opposite effect. You want to hold on to it. You want to stash it away because it might stop coming in. That's when you start to think twice about giving it away—to God or to anyone else.

But I also think that once I had money, that's when I really learned to manage it. Before I had a lot, there wasn't much choice; I just bought food or paid the most overdue bill. But once I had money, whether it was an extra hundred dollars in my pocket or an NFL contract, I had choices to make.

Sometimes I get distracted thinking about what everyone else is doing—like the guy who got the $46 million contract and is not tithing. He has an extra $4.6 million to spend. I know I'm not alone in those kinds of thoughts. No matter how big or small a man's paycheck, our culture tells him that he's worth what he makes. And the way to increase his value in the world is to buy more houses, cars, and jewelry.

Just last week I had a conversation with another player who collects expensive watches. He's always trying to get me to invest in something I don't need, like buying a private jet or collecting something expensive—the way Jay Leno collects cars. But I'm not into anything like that.

My temptations come in different ways. I look at my portfolio and think, *I'll be out of a job in two years. If I never work again, will this be enough to provide for my family? The interest alone from the money I gave the church could buy so much. . . .*

Occasionally I find myself thinking, *When is the rug going to be pulled out from under us? When is somebody going to say, "You don't belong here anymore. Get out"?*

There is a finite duration to my job. One day it will stop. And it will stop suddenly. All it takes is an injury. Even if I play injury free until I decide to retire, I'll still be young, with the rest of my life ahead of me. But I'll be unemployed.

Sometimes I have concerns about what I will do after football. That's where my faith comes in. I trust that God will open other doors for me to walk through. In fact, I've already seen some of that. During the off-season, there are a number of opportunities to make paid speeches. Sometimes I've been paid more than I felt I deserved. But that's God's blessing. I think he uses those opportunities to prepare me now for what will come next, after my professional sports career is over.

That's just one way my faith gives me perspective. God continually reminds me that he is active and present in my life now—just as he was when I didn't have money. So although I sometimes struggle with my thoughts, tithing is a rule for me. It's part of keeping first things first. There is no doubt I've been financially blessed, but I also realize that everything God has given me is for a reason and giving back is part of that reason.

I'm not afraid to ask for more money in contract negotiations—not that I need it, since I have certainly survived on a lot less—but I know God has a purpose for it. The more I make, the more I can give away. I believe all money is God's anyway, so when it is given to me, it is given with a responsibility to use it for his purposes. That's one of the reasons we started our First Things First Foundation. It's a way for us to share our blessings by blessing others.

So do I struggle when it comes to tithing? Yes, sometimes I do. But never to the point where I don't do it.

But here's what's ironic: Over time, I've learned there's great joy and a lot of fun in giving money away. I love being able to bless other people. There's real pleasure in sharing your blessings, and that's something I want to teach my kids.

The problem is, it's hard to teach your kids to find joy in giving something away that was never really theirs to begin with. They didn't do anything to earn the money, so when it goes out, they don't feel the sacrifice behind it. That's one of the reasons why Brenda and I find that teaching our kids to serve others is a better lesson at their ages. When they sacrifice their free time or have to get up to push a wheelchair, that sacrifice is their own; and when they see how their service blesses others, they own the joy that was created in the sacrifice. That's why we believe that serving others is such an important lesson for our children, and we'll talk more about it in the next chapter.

Money Changes Things

Although having money and sharing it is certainly a blessing, sometimes there's a darker side to that blessing. No one ever gave a thought to what Brenda and I did with our money when we didn't have much. But now that we have a lot, people have all kinds of ideas about what we should do with it.

When Brenda and I gave gifts to people before the big contract, they were always grateful to receive them. Now they often seem disappointed that what they've received isn't more. Everyone seems to have an opinion on what we should do with our money and how they fit into those plans. We've each had people ask us for financial help to one degree or another, implying that it is our responsibility to make their lives easier.

"If I were you and I had the money," they say, "I would give it."

Considering that the money most Americans spend on a new car could support a family in Africa for years, we all have the same opportunity to change lives. Yet the people that ask us to support them have very good reasons why they don't give all their money away. And so do we.

We also know it's much easier to say you'd give the money when it's not yours to give.

Brenda and I have learned that when we give any type of gift or do charity work, people have an expectation of what we should give. And unless we meet their expectations, it's never enough.

I never imagined that money would change our relationships as much as it has. And don't get me wrong. I want to help everyone, but I can't. And sometimes I shouldn't, because I know how much I learned about God when I had to depend on him to provide. The faith lessons I learned when I couldn't afford gas for the vomit-stained Jimmy taught me that God is my provider—at all times.

But now that I have more resources, I've learned new lessons about God and his character. For example, the Bible says—and we have learned firsthand—that loaning money changes a relationship. Brenda and I may not change, but the person we've loaned it to has new concerns that complicate the relationship.

Early on, we made mistakes when we loaned money. For example, we once had a borrower sign a contract with a repayment plan. We thought that having a business document would take the personal issues out of it, but when you loan money to people you know, it's always personal. That's one of life's rules. And it always changes things.

Here's the typical pattern: The borrowers are grateful for the loan, and for a few months, they make regular payments. Then they have trouble making the payments on time or can't make them at all. They apologize, but soon they're embarrassed about the situation. They start thinking we're mad at them, so they stop calling or coming over. What may have been a relationship among equals suddenly becomes one where they feel indebted to us.

That is never what we want to happen. We would much rather preserve the relationship than anything else. So there are times when people ask me for money and I want to say no. Not because I don't have it or I don't want to give it to them, but because I want to protect the relationship. The person asking usually doesn't think about how things will change, but because I've seen it happen so many times, I know it will.

Brenda and I have made plenty of mistakes when it comes to loaning money or giving gifts to people we know. And it isn't always the other person's fault. There have been times when Brenda and I have given money to someone who we thought really needed it, but the next time we saw them they had a new car, or they had just returned from an expensive vacation. We'd think, *How can they afford that?*

We've learned from our experiences, and our mistakes have cost us some priceless relationships. As a result, we no longer loan money. Now it's a rule that if we give someone money, it's a gift, with no strings attached. They don't have to tell us how they spent it, and we don't question what they did with it. Sometimes it's hard for us to step back and say, "Okay, here it is. Do what you want." But we let go of the money because we feel as if that's what God has called us to do.

{ BRENDA }

The first few times Kurt got a big check, he'd show it to me, and I'd be like, "Get out of here! Are you kidding me?" We compared it to my dad's earnings at John Deere. "This is four times what my dad would make in a year," or "My dad would have to work ten years to make that much money." We did that for a long time. It was our way of keeping things in perspective.

Occasionally, we still do stuff like that. Kurt will get paid $50,000 to speak for twenty minutes.

"Seriously? Nobody has anything to say that's worth that!"

"I feel like I just stole their money, like I didn't do enough to earn it," Kurt will respond.

But because he does a job that few people can do, and something our culture values so much, he gets paid well to do it. Still, sometimes it's hard not to feel guilty.

While we were in St. Louis, we often talked with our pastors about these feelings of guilt. "Receive the blessing," was their response. "No, maybe you don't think you deserve it, but understand that it comes from God. Receive it for what it is. A blessing."

There is no doubt that God blesses his people, and some of them, like Solomon, he blesses financially. But many people are not blessed financially. Kurt and I don't pretend to have all the answers—why God chooses who he chooses. We just know that our job is to be thankful for the blessings he's given us. The best way to show that thankfulness is by sharing what we have.

When we got our first big check, we gave each of our family members—brothers, sisters, and parents—a $10,000 check for Christmas. Over the next few years, we gave them things like TiVo subscriptions and full-length leather coats. I know that receiving those gifts blessed each of them as much as it blessed us to give them. But when we moved to Phoenix, it was right after Hurricane Katrina, and somehow, it didn't seem appropriate to give extravagant gifts when so many had so little. So that Christmas, we gave $10,000 to build a playground in a community affected by Katrina. That became our tradition for the next few years; every year we would make a donation on behalf of our family to a charity of our choice.

Recently, as I thought more about our rules and how we teach our kids to share their blessings, I realized that the joy of giving comes from seeing the difference your gift makes. When we gave on behalf of our family members, they weren't getting to experience that joy. So this year, we changed things a bit so they could see for themselves the differences their gifts made. This year, we gave each family a designated amount of money, and they got to choose which charity to give it to. That allowed them to share in the joy of giving too.

Money Conflicts

Even though we have more money than we've ever had, Kurt and I still disagree on how to use it to help others. As with most couples, money can cause trouble between us.

Fifteen years ago, when I was a single mom scraping together enough quarters to buy a Happy Meal, I would have told a couple arguing about such things, "Shut up! What do you two have to complain about? At least you have money!"

And I know our disagreements aren't the same as the ones between a John Deere employee and his wife, who may struggle—like my parents did—to pay their bills, but they're still significant to me. I've seen the different ways we've tried to handle money. Some of it has worked, and some of it hasn't. But through it all, I've seen how money can change people and change relationships, so I am very cautious about who we give money to and for what reasons.

If someone asks Kurt for money, he'll want to give them the shirt off his back. But I can think of all the reasons not to. Those reasons have nothing to with keeping it for ourselves and everything to do with the relationship.

"We gave them money last time, and it didn't help their problem," I'll say. Or I'll tell Kurt, "They need to learn to trust in God, not in you. The only way for that to happen is for them to struggle a bit."

In our experience, we've found that we learn the most when we struggle the most. I feel really strongly about that, and I'll passionately make my point. Kurt will listen to me. He will hear everything I say. He'll even concede that I have some brilliant—okay, he says "valid"—points. Then he will take off his shirt and give it away.

And I'm okay with that.

When I was little, I remember my mom giving money to a homeless man on the corner. "But what if he buys beer with it?" I asked.

"Once I give it, I'm not responsible for what he does," she said. In her heart, she felt that she was supposed to give that money, so she obeyed. What happened after that was the homeless man's choice.

That's how I feel when Kurt and I argue about giving away money. He works hard for it, and although we share everything, it's ultimately his decision where it goes. I'm thankful that he listens to me and takes my perspective into consideration. But ultimately, he has to obey what the Holy Spirit tells him to do.

What the recipient does with the money is between that person and God. Kurt and I can't worry about it. I trust that he is listening to those sacred promptings, and I let it go.

But, of course, there's an exception to every rule.

This past year, Kurt's contract negotiations with the Cardinals were not going well. They were offering about $10 million a year, which was less than Kurt had hoped for and less than the other top five quarterbacks in the league were making. As a result, Kurt became a free agent and began looking at offers from other teams. When the San Francisco 49ers showed interest and Kurt reciprocated that interest, fans and members of the media thought it was just a ploy to get more money. But I never thought that.

When the 49ers invited us to come for a visit, I thought that perhaps God wanted us to make a move. Though Phoenix was our home, it was the perfect time to uproot the kids if we were going to do it. Jesse would graduate in May, and though Zack could stay for a third senior year at his high school, we thought if we moved to San Francisco, he might be able to get a job working for the 49ers, picking up trash or something. The younger kids would all be in the same elementary school for the first time, so their adjustment would be easier. So, throughout the trip, Kurt and I talked about keeping our minds open.

As we flew back to Phoenix on the 49ers' private jet, Kurt asked, "What do you think?"

At the time, we believed the 49ers were offering Kurt $12 million a year—all guaranteed. That was 20 percent more than the $10 million the Cardinals had offered. "That's a serious offer," I told him. "It's also the perfect time for the kids to make a move. But it's your decision. I'm praying for you and for God's will to be clear."

I settled back into the leather seats and thought, *I could get used to this.*

I must have dozed off, because when I opened my eyes, forty-five minutes had passed. Kurt was staring at me.

How sweet, that man loves me so much, he even loves to watch me sleep.

"Whatcha thinking about?" I asked, digging for the compliment I knew was coming.

"God spoke to me."

"He did?" I sat up in my chair. "What did he say?"

"He told me to stay with the Cardinals, take less money, and give some of it away so we can keep Anquan Boldin."

Anquan Boldin was one of the Cardinals' top receivers and an instrumental part of the team's success last year. He also was in contract negotiations with the Cardinals, and the talks weren't going well.

"Kurtis Eugene! Are you kidding me?" I said. "I went to sleep at $12 million, and forty-five minutes later I wake up to $10 million and some of it going to another player? I am never going to sleep again!"

Though the Cardinals couldn't make the Boldin deal an official part of Kurt's contract, he ended up finalizing an agreement to stay with the team. It was Kurt's decision, and I trusted him to do the right thing. Again, it illustrates the point that after I say what I'm thinking, what Kurt does with this money is ultimately between him and God.

All this happened while I was working on this chapter. I have to say, it's kind of funny that God had me writing about "sharing the blessing" at the same time he was telling Kurt to live it out.

Though some people look at the money or the fame and are impressed by it, we've tried to teach our kids that money always comes with responsibilities. We have a responsibility to receive the money as a blessing, and we also have a responsibility to joyfully share it with others as God leads us to do so.

Even if I'm asleep when God speaks.

CHAPTER 10

serve others

{ KURT }

Before I tell you this story, you have to know how much
I hate to throw my name around. I'm not a celebrity who
drops his name so he can get a better table or move to the
front of the line. Sure, when someone offers, I don't refuse,
but I despise doing it myself. You might even call it one of
my rules.

That's probably why I remember one Thanksgiving in
St. Louis so well. As a family, we believe Thanksgiving is
another time for us to give back to the community. Usually,
during the week of Thanksgiving, we help serve meals to the
homeless. Sometimes it is actually on the holiday; other years
it's a day or two earlier. That particular year, we did it earlier
in the week, and when Thanksgiving Day arrived, we didn't
have any plans. Brenda didn't want to cook, and we hadn't
made any reservations, so we had to come up with another
plan and come up with it fast—the kids were getting hungry.

Brenda had heard on the radio about a good BBQ

restaurant that was open on Thanksgiving. So while she got herself and the kids ready, I looked up the number and called them.

"Can I make a reservation for my family for dinner?" I asked.

"We don't take reservations," said the guy on the other end, "but we're not real busy, so you can just come in."

I thanked him and hung up. But when I told Brenda, she wasn't sure that would work. "We've got all the kids, and they're hungry. I don't want to stand in line with all of them. Use your name."

Like I said, I hate that. I hate dropping my name. "He told me it wasn't real busy. We could just come in."

But she wouldn't go for that. "You know how that could change. It's Thanksgiving. Just call back and use your name."

She was right, of course. It was Thanksgiving; we had young kids; and standing in line while they were hungry was not going to be fun. I realized if I was ever going to drop my name, now would be the time. So I called the guy back.

"Hey, this is Kurt Warner. I really don't want to come in and wait around for a table. I know you don't usually do it, but could we please reserve a table for my family?"

"We're not real busy," he repeated. "There are plenty of tables open."

"Please, man, could you just hold one of them for us?"

The guy laughed and said, "Hold on a second." There was a pause while I assumed he was talking to someone in charge. Finally, he came back on the line and said, "We're not supposed to reserve tables, but just this once, for you, I'll try and do it."

"Can you give me directions?" I asked as I grabbed a pencil to write them down.

"You know we're in the food court, right?"

"The food court at the mall?"

Needless to say, I told the guy I was sorry and that we wouldn't be coming down.

I couldn't believe it. Brenda had made me use my name to make reservations *at the food court*.

That's an embarrassing story on several levels, but at the same time, I'm glad that humbling things like that happen. We're very privileged, and it's easy to lose sight of the real world when we stay in our little bubble. That's why I try to get my kids out of the bubble and put them in situations that will humble them or at least let them see there's a bigger world out there. It's so easy for us to think, *Somebody else is going to take care of that*. So we put our kids, and ourselves, in situations where we can't just be selfish, places where we have to be concerned with the people around us.

Although I am glad to be able to provide for my kids, I also want them to know we are not called to just stand back and be served—letting someone else take care of everything for us. One of our rules is that we're called to serve others.

Thanksgiving

One way we do that is by serving Thanksgiving dinner at the local rescue mission on the Monday before Thanksgiving. It's an opportunity for the kids to be exposed to people who aren't as fortunate as they are. We've done it so many times now that the kids each have their own jobs. Zack stands next to Brenda and passes out the rolls. Jada gives out the dessert. Jesse and Kade hand everyone a Bible and a new sweatshirt.

Although there are the obvious lessons—how fortunate we are and the importance of serving others—each year Brenda uses the opportunity to teach the kids other lessons as well. One year, we were scheduled to serve the dinner at seven. When the kids got home from school at three, they all wanted a snack, but Brenda wouldn't let them have one. We usually eat by five, but that's the time we got in the car for the hour-and-a-half drive to the shelter. By now the kids were really whining.

"I'm starved."

"My tummy hurts!"

Brenda just let them complain.

At the shelter, they each got busy doing their jobs. For the next hour and a half, they watched as the people came through their line, and each recipient was so grateful for the food.

After we finished serving, around nine o'clock, the kids got back in the van. Still, no one said a word about how hungry they were. Finally, Brenda started an incredible conversation with them about what it would feel like to be hungry *all* the time. At least we knew we'd get something to eat, but some of the people we served that evening had no idea where their next meal would come from.

We were parked next to a bench, and Brenda pointed it out to the kids. "That's the bed that one of those men will sleep on tonight," she said. Although it was only a glimpse, it helped the kids to visualize the struggles of some of the people we served.

As I mentioned, Jesse and Kade pass out Bibles and First Things First sweatshirts to every homeless person that comes through. Everyone can use a Bible, and the homeless are always in need of new clothes—the Phoenix winters aren't cold, but there are still days you need a sweatshirt. One year, though, some of the other workers grabbed sweatshirts for themselves. A few even grabbed enough to take home to their families.

Jesse couldn't believe it. Their actions shocked her. They disappointed her so much that she couldn't help getting angry. She felt it more than anyone else because she was the one who had to tell some of the homeless people that we'd run out of sweatshirts.

I was glad that she was so upset by the injustice. Often with our kids, we see the opposite behavior; they're the first to grab a piece of cake or grab the biggest piece. My hope is that after Jesse and Kade witnessed the unfairness of that situation, they'll think twice when they want to grab something. It's one of those lessons you're never sure they get, but you hope they'll be able to make the transition from seeing it happen to someone else to applying it in their own lives.

We want our kids to learn from real-life situations, and we don't hesitate to capitalize on those when they happen. Like the other day, we were on the way home from the store, and Elijah was playing with a toy in the car. Unfortunately, the toy broke while he was playing with it. But Kade immediately gave his toy to Elijah. When I saw that, I said, "We're going to Toys 'R' Us now. I am going to buy Kade something because of what he did." Then everyone watched while Kade picked out a new toy. So, although it was a reward for Kade, it was also a lesson for the other kids: Sometimes when you make a sacrifice, there are unforeseen rewards.

Of course, I knew there'd be times during the next week when each of them would think they deserved something. And I was right. They would come up and tell me something good they had done or something they had sacrificed, and I would say, "That was awesome. Way to go! I'm so glad you did that."

Then they'd say, "Well, do I get something, like Kade?"

And I would tell them, "No, you just did what you were supposed to do."

"Well, Kade got—"

"I know what Kade got. And I wanted to bless him because of what he did."

They don't always understand the randomness of the rewards, but the randomness is intentional. I don't want them doing the right thing because they always expect to be rewarded—they won't be. I want them to do the right thing because it's simply the right thing to do. But sometimes the rewards serve to make the point as well.

With so many kids, those teachable moments happen all the time. Say there's one ice-cream sandwich left and two kids want it. They have to work it out. It's interesting to watch. When you know our kids, you know which one is going to give it up for the other. We applaud the sacrifice, but we also teach the other child, "Did you see that he gave the last one to you even though he wanted it?"

When we see the kids sacrificing for others, we praise

serve others

them. We eventually want them to be proactive about sacrificing for others and not just wait until a need appears. We want them to walk into a room and say, "How can I help? How can I make something easier on someone else?"

Jesse and I had a conversation about that the other day. The night before, I was taking care of all the kids, and things were a bit crazy. "You were doing nothing, and I had all the kids, and I wanted your help," I told her.

She knows that one of our rules is if you need something you have to ask for it, so she said, "Well, you didn't ask me to help."

Kids always find the loopholes, but she had missed the point. "I know I didn't *ask* you to help. And I didn't *need* your help. It wasn't that I couldn't handle it on my own. It's just that I want you to have an attitude and the wherewithal to say, 'How can I help?'"

It's not often in a child's nature to think of other people first, so we try to instill that in them. I know a lot of families do Bible studies and devotionals together. We really don't do that. Instead, we try to show them Jesus practically. That's also what I do when I'm speaking somewhere. Corporations are always suspicious that if I come speak to their employees, I'm going to stand at the podium and hit them with Bible verses, but really, all I do is show them the practical ways I live out these biblical principles.

Jesus is a great example of someone who was always serving others. That's why I think it is so important that I am intentional about giving my kids opportunities to do the same. I want them to see what serving looks like outside of their bubble and in the real world. And it's also a great reminder to me that that's what I need to do too.

{ BRENDA }

I remember when Kurt first said he wanted to start a charitable foundation; I didn't even know what that meant. I'd never heard of a foundation. I didn't grow up doing charity work. In my world, you just lived paycheck to paycheck and did your thing. When I found out that a foundation meant giving money away, I thought, *It's our money! Why would we want to do that?*

But Kurt, in typical fashion, didn't want to do a foundation like other people did foundations—they write a few checks and get a statement at the end of the year. Kurt, of course, wanted to do it better than anyone else. He wanted us to actually be involved in the foundation—to use it as a practical way of living out our faith. So our foundation is all about serving others.

It was the second-best decision he's ever made. The first, of course, was marrying me.

The foundation has allowed us to fund underserved areas of the communities we've lived in and to do so based on our own experiences and interests. For example, one cold morning I was driving in St. Louis; I passed a bus stop and saw a little kid wearing a Windbreaker. It was the middle of winter, and the kid didn't have a proper coat. I thought, *How many other kids don't have warm coats for winters in St. Louis?*

I found out—thousands of kids don't have the necessary protection from the winter cold.

So, as a part of our First Things First Foundation, we started a coat drive. Now, eight years later, 100,000 coats have been donated and distributed. And it happened just because I drove past that bus stop, noticed another person's struggle, and was in a position to do something about it.

Another time while we were still in St. Louis, a Boy Scout troop came to visit Rams Park. Kurt, of course, met all the Scouts, took pictures with the troop, and signed autographs before he left for minicamp. A few days later, one of the boys from the troop was killed while visiting the St. Louis Zoo with his first grade class. He was hit by a drunk driver while standing outside the zoo.

He was seven years old.

I went to the boy's funeral because I knew he was a fan of Kurt's and Kurt was still away at the minicamp. Although I didn't know anyone at the funeral, I could still feel the tremendous grief. But what most saddened me was seeing the casket. I'd never seen a child's casket before, and it broke my heart. It was just this itty-bitty casket.

Zachary could have been in a little casket when he was four months old. He could have died, and I could have been the mother at her little boy's funeral. I thought about how the parents had had to go out and buy that casket, and I thought about how blessed I was that Zack had lived and how I'd never had to go through that. On the way home from the funeral, I called Marci, who runs our foundation, and said, "We've got to do something. I don't want grieving parents to have to buy a casket for their child."

Since then, through our Little Angels casket program, if

a child Zack's age or younger is accidentally killed in St. Louis, we donate money toward the purchase of a casket. The family doesn't know it's from us, but it's one of the little things we started through our foundation, based on our own personal interests and the needs that touched our hearts.

Of all the programs we do, I think the one I most closely identify with is our Home for the Holidays program. Through our foundation, we partner with Habitat for Humanity and similar programs to identify needy families that are scheduled to move into their new homes around a holiday.

As a single mom, I've lived in low-income housing where the rental home didn't have any closets and the floors were so uneven that the push toys and balls rolled to the front of the house every night. I understand how important it is for families to own their own homes, and I can relate to the families we help.

Once the house is built, but before the family moves in, we work with sponsoring companies to completely furnish the inside. We do everything from arranging the brand-new furniture that has been donated to lighting the candles that sit on top of a new table. We put newly donated appliances in the kitchen and fill the refrigerator with food. Our sponsors provide a washer and dryer and then make sure there is laundry detergent and dryer sheets to be used in it. There are new beds with new pillows and new pillowcases. We even have sponsors who provide a computer for the family.

The recipients—often single parents—have no idea that all this has been done. They think the house is empty. When they open the door, they are so overwhelmed that they just start shaking, often crying or screaming with joy. Each time I see that, I feel the old emotions all over again, because that's exactly how I would have felt if someone had done that for me and my kids.

Later that day, when we have dinner with our kids and talk about the best part of our day, I'll tell them what happened. I'll say something like, "Today a single mom who raises two boys just your age got a house full of stuff. Do you know what the boys were most excited about? The lawn mower, so they could mow their first lawn, because that's what boys like to do." So our experiences helping those families have normal lives can be ways to teach our own kids about what having a normal life means.

Everything we do in our foundation starts with something that's significant to Kurt or me. Like our Disney weeks. Growing up, I never went to Walt Disney World because we couldn't afford a trip like that. The best we could do was to drive ten hours south to Arkansas, where we stayed with relatives and they cooked for us. Then we drove back home. That was our spring break. Our Christmas break. Our summer vacation.

Kurt and I wanted to provide a trip to Disney World for kids who otherwise wouldn't be able to go. So, through our foundation, we partner with organizations like Make-A-Wish and Dream Factory to make two of their most requested dreams come true—meeting a celebrity and visiting Walt Disney World. For many of those families, it's the only family vacation they've had since their child was diagnosed with a life-threatening illness. Sadly, it may also be the last one they have together.

It's a chance for the kids and their parents and other family members to be normal for a week. Each day we spend several hours at the park with them. During their stay, they get to go to the front of the line. They think that's pretty cool—and so do my kids. We also give them time to spend together as a family during the day. And there is usually a pool party one night.

The families stay at Give Kids the World Village, a resort that was specially designed for kids with life-threatening illnesses. At some point during the week, the volunteers—some of whom are our own kids—watch the sick children while Kurt and I meet with the parents. I know what it's like to be told that your child is not going to make it, so I understand some of what those parents are going through. Every time we go to one of those parent meetings, the parents just weep, because they finally get connected with other families who face the same things they do. They're all in the same boat, and it's not fair. They'd do anything to take the illness away.

We sit around and get to know their stories, because everybody's got a story. There was one family who had never taken a family vacation. For one week, they didn't have to pay for anything, and they could just enjoy each other's company and have a few laughs. Kurt and I know how much we enjoy a night out without the kids, so when we found out there was a couple who had never been out on a date since their child was diagnosed, we did something about it. During the Disney week, staff was on hand to help them finally have a night alone, and it changed their marriage.

One day I pushed around a little boy in a wheelchair. He didn't like to be touched much, but if I rubbed my cheek up against his, he would calm down. I'll never forget that.

The first few years, we just took our kids along so they could have fun. But now the older ones go as volunteers. Jesse, for example, has to be attached to someone at all times so she can help children with their medications, push the wheelchairs, carry the oxygen tanks, and ride on the rides with them. She loves being able to love on those kids. Every year, my kids fall in love with the kid they are helping. They're like BFFs all of a sudden, and that is so great to see.

I understand that feeling. I feel it every year when we go to Disney, but I also feel it every week when I get to hold my babies.

While I was in St. Louis, I started holding sick babies at the hospital, and now I do it in Phoenix. Kurt loves it because it doesn't draw any media attention; it's just something I volunteer to do where no one really knows or cares who I am. I'm just a volunteer who wants to hold babies. When I started doing it in St. Louis, it was one of those things that balanced out the whirlwind of the Super Bowl stuff. And I fell in love with it. It's one way I can be God's hands here on earth.

In Phoenix, I've invited several of the players' and coaches' wives to join me; so now about seven or eight of us go each week and just sit and rock the babies.

Last week, Kurt went with me for the first time, and he got to meet all the babies I had been talking about—babies like Keenan and Delilah. Because Kurt always sings "Hey There Delilah" when he's trying to beat Jesse on American

Idol Wii (which he has never done), I told him to sing it to the baby. But there were too many people around, so he wouldn't do it. Guess it's an image thing.

People ask if I do those things through the foundation to teach our kids a lesson. The answer is yes. One of our rules is that our kids need to serve others. And Kurt and I will keep doing these kinds of projects for the kids, hoping they get what we're trying to teach. Of course, we won't know for sure until they're adults and they're serving on their own.

But there's another reason why I do it. A more important one. I personally involve myself in the work of the foundation because of the joy it brings. There is nothing like watching a single mom walk into her first house, fall to her knees, and cry out in joy.

Selfishly, that is also my beautiful moment, the one that I get to be a part of. I want to keep feeling what that feels like. It's also what I want my kids to feel. I want them to know they can make a difference in the world, and then feel how good it feels.

◁ Our wedding day was bittersweet. The front pew where my parents should have been sitting was empty, but I also knew that marrying Kurt meant I had found a partner for life who would love me as unconditionally as my parents had.

▽ In my senior year of college at the University of Northern Iowa, I finally got to play football. It was nice to have the support of my dad and my brother Matt at my games.

◁ PFC Brenda Carney (second from the left). I was in the top two of my graduating class. I knew I was going to work in Intelligence, but I wasn't sure what that meant. I thought I was going to be an international spy.

and so it began…

Brenda loves lying out at the beach, but I don't.
Here she buried me in the sand so I couldn't
move—just so she could stay out longer.

Kurt doesn't like posing for family photos. ▷
During a break in this photo shoot when the kids
ran off to jump on the trampoline, I grabbed Kurt's
face and kissed him so he wouldn't run off too.
The photographer took the picture
when we weren't looking.

◁ This is a picture of my
parents, Jenny Joe and
Larry Carney. It was
taken when I was in
the seventh grade and
we were posing for
family photos. What
I love is that my mom
was grabbing my
dad's face, just like I
grabbed Kurt's in the
picture above.

let's make out!

Zack was my buddy from the first day I met him. ▷
Though Brenda and I were only dating and I hadn't
yet become Zack's dad, we were having a great time
together, laughing and loving each other.

◁ Zack and me taking a
walk on the beach in
Hawaii after the 2009
Pro Bowl. I think it's
great that we're still
buddies, and that he
still wants to hold
my hand.

As a mom, I love seeing Zack's playful side. ▷
He is always in the moment, always happy, and
always trying to get others to share in his joy.
In this picture, he made me go down the slide
with him, making us the two biggest kids
on the playground. But we didn't care;
we were having too much fun.

zachary taylor

I tell Jesse that she looks like me, but she doesn't believe it—even though everyone tells her it's true. Then she sees us together in a picture, and she can't deny it. This picture is my proof.

Jesse loving on Kade after a Pop Warner football game. She's the proud big sister, but he doesn't want to be kissed!

This is Jesse and me on her seventeenth birthday. ▷
She'll soon be leaving the nest and
flying on her own at college.

jesse jo

◁ Kade has Kurt's good looks and charm. (I can't help it; I'm a proud mama.) We hope he's learning the lessons we're trying to teach him, so that one day he'll grow to be a man who has his dad's character, too.
▽

kade eugene

I tried to make a rule at our house that we would have ice cream for supper one night a week. This is Jada and me picking out supper—before Brenda put an end to the rule.

Jada loves to cheer, ▷ and I love seeing her command attention when she's performing onstage with her squad. I'm still uncomfortable with her wearing all that makeup—she's only eight. I want Jada to know that she's beautiful on the inside, not because of how she looks, but because of who she is.

jada jo

Elijah wears his hair in a Mohawk because his ▷
favorite football player, Larry Fitzgerald, told him
it looked good that way. We took this picture at
the Pro Bowl in 2009 when we realized that now
Elijah is even starting to dress like Larry!

▽ I tell new moms to always have their camera out
so that it's accessible when the moments happen.
Here Kade is roughhousing with Elijah. But what
Kade doesn't know is that, as he tears into his
little brother, Elijah is enjoying every minute of it.

This was another unplanned moment I ▽
caught because my camera was accessible.
At our house in Cabo, Kurt becomes a
human diving board. The kids climb on
him and then jump into the pool. Here
he's putting a little muscle into it.

elijah storm

Cherishing every minute with the Babygirls. This was one of the last times I was able to hold both girls in my arms at the same time. They grow up so fast!

△ The whole family loves to hang out at the pool, even the Babygirls. Sienna has never been afraid of the water. She was completely independent at the age of three, when she could jump off the board and swim across the pool.

◁ I can still hold both girls at the same time. It won't be long before they're too big for even me to hold them both. But that doesn't mean I'm willing to let them go....

sienna rae

Sierra is the youngest and the smallest, but she's also the one who makes the most noise. She's spicy, like her mama. When I am home, she loves to hang on me. I hope she always will.

Sierra was watching ▷ TV, and Sienna came up and put her arm around her. I grabbed my camera and got this shot of Sienna loving and protecting her smaller twin sister.

Have we mentioned that none of the kids likes football? ▷ Here's Sierra posing for pictures rather than watching a game. Not only does she like to pose, but she also worries about her hair and clothes. She's a little fashionista.

sierra rose

Elijah, Jada, and Kade hanging out at the pool.

Brenda had this ▷ picture taken as a Father's Day surprise when I played for the Rams. Not only are the kids wearing jerseys, but they also have on ice packs and Ace bandages so they can "look like Daddy."

the whole team

This picture not only shows the whole family, but it also shows how **each** child is different. Zack is reaching down to splash Jesse, who is pulling **away** but enjoying it. Kade is telling Jada not to get him wet, while she kicks **up** the water, completely soaking herself. Elijah's trying to avoid getting **splashed**, while the twins belly laugh and try to see who can kick up the most water.

{ PHOTO BY ANDREWGRANTPHOTO.COM }

Through our foundation, we do an event with Special Olympics called the Punt, Pass, and Kick clinic. Brenda and I create an obstacle course and help the athletes run through it. At the finish, they get to jump on the mat. This picture is of us doing the touchdown dance with one of the athletes.

After I saw a child shivering at a bus stop, ▷ I wanted to do something about it. Through our foundation, we started a coat drive. Here I'm collecting coats from fans before a Rams game. More than 100,000 coats have been donated since we began the program.

◁ I spent weeks in the hospital with Zack after his injury, so I know what it's like for a family with a sick child. That's why Kurt and I set up the Baskets of Hope program through our foundation. We take Bibles, toys, music, journals, and other goodies to pediatric hospitals when we make visits.

first things first

I started holding babies at Ranken Jordan Pediatric Hospital in St. Louis. Kaylee was born at 24 weeks, but she's now in the second grade. Not only did I fall in love with her, but so did Kurt and our kids.

During one of our ▷ Baskets of Hope visits, the parents of this brave little girl asked me to pray with her.

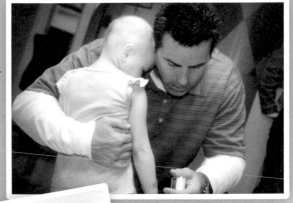

◁ Each year, Brenda and I host a weeklong trip to Disney World for up to ten families with a child in medical crisis. Our kids serve as volunteers, and the families draw strength from each other. Here we're showing off our "guns."

As a former single mom, ▷ nothing makes me happier than seeing another single mom move into her first home. Through our foundation and sponsors, we surprise parents by furnishing their new houses—everything from furniture and appliances to food in the cupboards.

◁ At Disney, waiting for the parade to start. My hands are full with the Babygirls, and Kurt is trying to calm Elijah, who is afraid Mickey might show up.

Game nights are always ▽ fun at our house, though sometimes mixing creative kids with competitive kids means not everyone is happy with the results.

When taking family pictures of nine people, it's hard to get everyone to focus on the same thing. At the beach in Florida, we solved it by turning our backs to the camera.

The shoes are all kept ▷ in the entryway near the garage. We call this the "ugly-way," and only those closest to us get to see it. Everyone else uses the front door, the "pretty-way."

▽ This oversized calendar serves as the organizational control center of the house. Without it, we'd live in chaos—or maybe this is evidence of the chaos!

My workout room has ▷ family photos lining the walls and a great view of the backyard. But sometimes I have to remove the stuffed animals and shopping carts before I can work out.

a day in the life

This picture shows our similarities and our differences. At the same time, it shows how we're not complete unless we're all together. I try to organize this same photo once a year when I can find matching and stain-free clothes for everybody. Then I have to talk Kurt into it.

CHAPTER 11

marriage rules

{ KURT }

One of the things I love most about Brenda is that she will always say exactly what she's thinking. Whether she's arguing about giving money to a friend or telling you what she thinks about George Bush's ear hair, you will never have to ask her, "What do you really think?" You will always know.

That's also one of the rules in our marriage: Brenda will tell me what she thinks, whether I want to hear it or not. When you're in a career like mine, it's easy to get full of yourself—or, on the contrary, down on yourself—based on your current performance. Brenda is the person in my life who always reminds me of the truth of who I am, not what I do.

I'm fortunate to have someone like her. Often, celebrities are surrounded by yes-men and yes-women, and they lose perspective or touch with reality. Having an honest voice that I can trust—from someone who loves me—helps keep me from making mistakes I might otherwise make. That's why, even when I disagree, I often do what she says. It's not

159

a power thing; it's a wisdom thing. Brenda often sees things more clearly than I do.

Every marriage has rules—whether they are clearly articulated to both partners or not. Some rules are practical, such as who pays the bills or who takes out the trash. Others come about from necessity, like how much is okay to spend without talking with your spouse first. Some are meant to protect the marriage, like rules about if and when you can be alone with the opposite sex. Others are rules that you wish were followed but often aren't.

Brenda and I have our own list of rules that we both agree on. But if I could, I would add a few lighthearted rules of my own for her:

1. Brenda should turn off the TV before she falls asleep, because I can't sleep with it on.
2. She should put away the milk when she's done with it, because I hate warm milk.
3. I hate climbing over her clothes—she needs to pick them up more often.
4. I should be able to watch *SportsCenter* every once in a while, instead of always being forced to watch her shows—*Dancing with the Stars, Brothers and Sisters, Desperate Housewives*, and *Oprah.*

Those are small things that annoy me—and perfect opportunities to create rules for Brenda to follow. But that's probably not going to happen, because in our marriage, rules aren't about making the other person less annoying or creating perfect behavior. For us, the rules are ways to talk about the expectations we have for each other. Choosing which rules we follow is based on what really matters to the other person. Although warm milk is annoying—and some days *really* annoying—ultimately, it's not a deal breaker for our marriage.

Other rules really do matter. They matter because they're very important to one of us or because they protect our marriage. For example, one of the things we do is have all of our e-mail come into the same account. That allows us to see each other's e-mail exchanges. Not only can we monitor the correspondence, but it keeps us accountable as we send out our own messages.

I have an e-mail list of about one hundred or so people with whom I have a cyber Bible study. Frequently, sometimes as often as weekly during the off-season, I send out a letter to the whole list—usually discussing what God is teaching me. People on the list often reply to me directly about something I wrote, and usually I respond privately to that person. As a result, the exchange becomes a personal correspondence with a particular individual. In most cases, it's harmless enough— just give-and-take over the content of my original e-mail. Occasionally, however, Brenda will say something about one of those e-mails. Sometimes it's a comment in jest: "Oh, is that your girlfriend again?" Other times, she warns me of things I may not see: "Be careful how you respond to her. Something's not right." And she cautions me about letting my responses get too personal.

Once or twice, she has even asked me to stop

corresponding with someone. To me, it might seem as if the responder is talking directly about the content of my e-mail. But I trust that my wife sees something that I don't, so I cut off the personal correspondence, or I only respond when I'm writing to the entire group. That isn't something Brenda and I spend a lot of time discussing; most of the time, it's not even something she asks from me. It's just something I do to honor her. If she mentions her concern, I make the necessary adjustment.

Is the threat real or imagined?

Does it matter?

I know there have been moments when I've felt jealous. It didn't matter to me whether it was real or imagined. And so it doesn't matter to me if I see the same thing Brenda's seeing. My experience has been that she often sees things develop before I do. So whether it's there or not there doesn't really matter to me. Because I want to protect my marriage and honor my wife, discontinuing an e-mail correspondence is a simple thing I can do for us. It's just not a huge deal, especially when I plan to spend the rest of my life with Brenda.

The Billy Graham Rule

One of the people who really influenced my thinking in this area was evangelist Billy Graham. I spoke at one of his events in St. Louis, but before I did, I happened to read that he did everything he could to avoid the appearance of wrongdoing. He always kept his office door open, never met with a female alone, and if he was alone in an elevator and a woman got on, he'd get off and catch the next one so it wouldn't be just the two of them. He avoided even the appearance of something inappropriate—not only to protect himself but also to protect the women he worked with.

Apparently it worked. Despite his celebrity, despite the travel and the late hours I'm sure he put in, there has never been even a hint of scandal during his many decades of service. Billy Graham is a man who always honored his wife. Billy loved Ruth enough to keep those rules for her—but I bet he'd say they were as much for his own benefit as they were for hers.

Not long after I spoke at the Graham event, Brenda and I began to add rules to our marriage. I remember one of the first was that I wouldn't drive the babysitter home alone. We call it our Billy Graham rule: Avoid even the appearance of wrongdoing.

In retrospect, we were really wise to make this a rule. Over the years, there have been a string of accusations against celebrities who were accused of sleeping with the babysitter or the nanny. True or false, the allegations damaged relationships and reputations. That's one of the reasons why we're so careful. Even the hint of a scandal has the potential to hurt those we love. That's why the rules are so important. We think they've protected us from ever being in a similar situation.

Betsy, our current nanny, has three kids of her own and has been happily married for twenty-five years. Betsy and her husband, Rory, who also works part-time for us, have been friends of ours since my Arena Football days. Their friendship has been a real blessing to us. In the past, we've had young women help out around the house, and I know that's been a concern for Brenda. It's not that she didn't trust me, but she didn't always trust them. They weren't always thoughtful in the way they acted or dressed.

In Chicago, I have a female marketing director who works for me. Whenever Julie sets up an event, we have to make sure there's another man along, or we'll ride to the event separately. Brenda and I both know that Julie's a professional, but it's an appearance thing. If I'm at an event and a woman is sitting next to me, people will automatically assume she's my wife. If they find out she's not, we don't want them to be misled into thinking something that isn't true.

It's funny; Brenda used to be so recognizable with her gray spiky hair. Now that her hair is long and blonde, I'm sure some people have said, "Who's that blonde with Kurt?" In fact, it even happened once with a friend of ours. She came up to Brenda and me on the street, started talking, and then said, "How's Brenda doing?"

I said, "She's right here. Why don't you ask her?"

It was a funny moment, but to Brenda and me it was a reminder of why we both follow the rules. What if that woman had gone home and told everyone she had seen Kurt Warner with a woman other than his wife? It would still have been funny when she learned the truth, but in the meantime, how many people would have come to the wrong conclusion?

One other time, when we were traveling as a family, Brenda and I boarded the plane first, and Jesse boarded a few minutes later. As our daughter walked through the first class section, she heard one guy say to another, "Dude, I am telling you, that was not Kurt Warner's wife!"

Unfortunately, even an unfounded rumor can do a lot of damage when you have a high-profile career. The media love to build people up and then find a reason to take them down—it makes good television and talk-show conversation. Because I've made such a public stance about my faith, even a hint of impropriety has serious consequences for my image in the media. One slip and they'd pounce on it.

But more important, what if our kids heard something? Especially if it were untrue? Children often think that newspapers and TV are always reliable sources of information. How do you explain to your child that the anchorman was just reporting a rumor? We don't ever want to find out, which is why we think the rules are so important. They protect us from even the appearance of wrongdoing.

Of course, the rules aren't just for me. There have also been times when I've been jealous of things I've heard Brenda say or watched her do. I'll overhear her and her girlfriends talking about how some guy is good-looking, and I'll think, *Why is she saying that? I'd never get away with saying that about another woman.*

I've also seen times when she's made a connection with another guy. I won't call it flirting—that's going too far. But whether she recognized it or not, I could see she connected with him in a way that if she and I weren't together or if I died or something, I could see the two of them developing something more.

In these situations, I tend to be less vocal than Brenda, which probably isn't good. But I don't want her to get upset about something when it's just me being paranoid. On the other hand, Brenda is more likely to say something anyway, thinking that if there is even a remote potential that something could develop in the future, it's better that we both have a warning so we can work to guard against it.

And she's right to speak up. We don't always see what the other person is seeing, so when one spouse calls attention to it, it can help both of us to be more cautious. That's why it's so important to have rules that we agree on for our marriage. Just because we don't see something in ourselves doesn't mean it's not there.

{ BRENDA }

Kurt gave you a little list of rules he'd like me to follow, but I think he forgot to mention the one he'd like me to follow more than any other. He'd probably go so far as to say it's an unwritten rule for every guy in every marriage: He'd like to have sex more frequently. Like all good rules, I think it's one of those things that must be negotiated between spouses.

But I also have an extra set of rules I'd like for Kurt to follow:

1. For starters, don't talk while you're brushing your teeth. As a nurse, I can deal with just about anything—poop, vomit, blood, you name it— but I can't deal with saliva. Even when I watch a movie and the star is brushing his teeth and starts talking, I start to gag. Kurt has known this almost as long as he's known me, yet he still talks to me when he brushes his teeth.

2. The water must be running while he brushes his teeth or while he helps the kids with theirs. I know that's not the environmentally conscious way to do it, but I can't stand the sound of people brushing their teeth. See rule #1.
3. I would like for Kurt to learn to cook something other than eggs and French toast. He says it doesn't matter because he only cooks when I'm not there.
4. I wish he would cook when I'm around.

I know those are silly things, and if our past is any indicator, I also know I'll spend the rest of my life gagging while he's brushing his teeth, and he'll spend the rest of his life drinking warm milk. But as Kurt mentioned, we have other rules that are more serious and that we're intentional about following.

You may remember that our first big fight was over Kurt's attending a bachelor party that included strippers. We would have broken up for good if my mother hadn't talked me into forgiving him. And I did. But on the way home from the wedding that night, I told him I deserved better. If he wanted to attend parties where there were naked women, then I wasn't the woman for him. That was when he first learned that we needed rules we could both agree on if our relationship was to continue.

What I knew that Kurt didn't yet know was that there are a lot of temptations, and even the most well-meaning person can fall for them if he or she isn't careful. Did I think Kurt was going to hook up with a stripper that night at the bachelor party? If you had asked me to place bets on it, I would have said no. But I also knew that if he sat and watched underdressed or undressed women for an hour, he wouldn't be able to leave those thoughts at the party. They would come home with him and come into bed with me. I don't want thoughts of another woman in my bedroom.

Kurt also needed to know that I required a high level of trust in my marriage. For me, attending a party with strippers significantly damaged that trust. Kurt knew he could throw out that rule, but he also knew that in doing so, he'd throw away the relationship. Fortunately, he didn't let that happen.

Over the years, a lot of rules have been added to "Don't go to parties where there are naked women." Most of them Kurt fully agrees with. There are others he doesn't understand, and some that he even disagrees with. Someday, maybe I'll let a therapist have a heyday figuring out all my issues, but in the meantime, the rules work both ways. Sometimes I don't understand why Kurt wants me to do certain things, or I'll think a rule doesn't really apply in a certain situation. But you know what? We follow them anyway, out of love for each other and as a way of protecting our marriage. Neither one of us loses anything because we set high standards or have lots of rules, but the opposite can be true. Without rules, we could lose a lot—worldly things like endorsements and reputations, but also more important things, like our spouse's trust.

One time, Kurt was on a game show and was teamed up with a female contestant. They wore matching jerseys and worked together to win money. I watched the show and didn't think anything of it. About a week later, a bouquet of flowers arrived with a note saying how much this woman had enjoyed getting to know Kurt—and she included her cell phone number. I couldn't help but be suspicious of her motives. Why would she think that Kurt would want to contact her?

Then I thought about some of the conversations I've overheard in the past. Like one on an elevator. We were at one of Kurt's away games, and I was staying in the same hotel as the team. As I got on the elevator, I heard a group of women talking about who on the team they wanted to hook up with that night. Of course, they didn't know who I was. But I was surprised at how brazen these women were. I knew there was a reputation that professional athletes have women in every city, but before I was an athlete's wife, I thought it was the players who encouraged it. Joining the NFL showed me you didn't have to be a "playa" to have women throwing themselves at you.

Anyone who is around the league knows how bold some of these women can be. That's why I am not the only one who has rules. The Cardinals won't let women onto the team floor. That includes wives. Not only can I not go to Kurt's hotel room; I can't even get on his floor. And that's because, over time, those in charge have learned that it's not always the athletes who are the problem; sometimes it's the women who are stalking their prey and then moving in for the kiss.

So that's what was going through my mind when Game Show Girl sent Kurt flowers with her phone number. I didn't think he had done anything wrong, but I was concerned he might be prey. "Just how comfortable did you make her feel?" I asked him.

Kurt thought I was accusing him of something more. "The only time I saw her was on the show."

"I realize that," I said. "But for some reason, she felt close enough to you to think it was okay to send you her cell phone number. Some women are just looking to see more in a situation than what's really there, and that means sometimes you're going to have to make other people feel uncomfortable to make sure they get the point."

Of course, my past plays into those things, making me more suspicious than others might be in similar circumstances. But I also believe that my concerns have protected us, our marriage, and our ministry. Kurt does too.

We've seen the tabloids take pictures of NFL players and other celebrities and publish them out of context, making the situation look like something it wasn't. To avoid that happening with us, one of the things that Kurt always tries to do is keep his arms at his sides while photos are taken of him. In the early days, when his celebrity was still a new thing for him, people would naturally put their arms around him, forcing him to do the same. These people were complete strangers to Kurt, but the appearance is that both parties know each other better than they do. You never know what someone is going to do or say with a picture like that. Nowadays, a woman has to be really determined if she wants to put her arm around Kurt for a picture. Sure, there are women who still try, but Kurt does his best to keep his arms at his sides just to avoid taking a misleading picture.

I guess if I had to summarize how we approach our rules, I'd say that we both think our marriage is a priority. Putting our marriage first protects our family, our ministry, and in many ways, Kurt's career. So we don't just let it happen. We're intentional about creating barriers that prevent our marriage from being attacked. Our rules are one way that we do it.

We've also learned that we're not always the best judges of our own behavior and feelings. Kurt is often naive about how risky things can be, and I'm often too suspicious. That's why we rely on each other to balance things out. In the end, this is one of those areas where, as Billy Graham demonstrated, it pays to be cautious. There is a lot at risk.

Fortunately, not all of our marriage rules are super serious. While writing this chapter, I asked Kurt to name some of the other rules I want him to adhere to. Here's what he said:

1. Always know when Brenda has a hair appointment so I can compliment her hair when she gets home.
2. When we're getting ready to go out, always say, "Wow!" as soon as Brenda walks down the stairs.
3. Tell her that she's beautiful, even though she's not going to believe me.

After he mentioned the first two, I called him a dork. But he's right about the third one. I'm glad he recognizes it as a rule, because he rarely follows it, though I would like him to. If I've gotten ready for whatever we're doing, taken the time to shower, put on makeup, squeezed into my Spanx, and worn something he will like, the first time he sees me I want him to go, "Wow!"

Often when I'm getting ready to leave the house, he's busy doing something else. So when he sees me, he's preoccupied. He may think I look nice, but he doesn't say anything until later—if at all. When I come downstairs, I want him to stop what he's doing and say it the first time he sets his eyes on me.

But my needs are not limited to when we're going out. I want him to tell me I am beautiful all the time. When we first started getting a lot of attention from the media, people said I looked like Kurt's mother, like Cloris Leachman, or like Alice from *The Brady Bunch*. That was a serious blow to my ego. Alice from *The Brady Bunch*? Now that my hair isn't short and spiky, bloggers are more likely to describe me as his "hot wife" rather than his mother, but I still need lots of reassurance some days. And although Kurt's right—I don't believe it when he says I'm beautiful—I still want him to say it. And he does. But like so many of our rules through-out this book, Kurt is more likely to observe it through his actions rather than just talk.

For example, when we get together, the first place he touches me is on my belly roll. What guy does that? "Love your belly roll," he'll say. I don't know if he loves it because I've given him seven kids or because he's trying to convince me I'm beautiful. But each time he does it, I am amazed that he's not bothered by it. Instead, he loves it, and it shows me how much he loves me.

We took vows when we got married, and those won't change. But our rules are subject to changes, additions, and deletions as we experience new things and as the world around us changes. We use the rules as a way to communicate our expectations about ourselves, each other, and our marriage. Ultimately, the rules are there to protect us and to make us better as a couple.

And sometimes, they're just a useful reminder that Kurt thinks I'm beautiful.

CHAPTER 12

One A Day
plus vitamins

{ **KURT** }

Training camp takes me away from my wife and kids for an
entire month, and I miss them like crazy. They're on my mind
every day, but the day that camp breaks, they're all I can think
about—especially Brenda. One time, as we were in our final
meeting before breaking camp, some of the guys talked about
what they couldn't wait to do when they got home—sleep in
their own beds or eat at their favorite restaurants. One guy
said, "About forty-five minutes after I get home, I'm gonna
get lucky."

That's what had been on my mind as well, so I yelled back
at him, "I'll race ya!"

I know my teammates assume that I have sex with my
wife, but I'm also sure many of them think that as an old
married couple and as Christians, we always do it at the same
time, in the same way, and always with the lights out. They
don't think that sex can be as fun for married couples as it
is for single people. But the truth is—it's more fun when

you're married because you have to be more creative. When Brenda and I were young, we just had to worry about her parents catching us. Now that we have seven little people and a nanny, it's more complicated and requires more ingenuity.

We don't mind talking about sex—it's an important part of our marriage. But for some reason, people are surprised when the subject comes up. But what's wrong with talking about sex? I'm a normal married guy with normal inclinations. Plus, my wife is hot.

I know some of my single teammates think that if you've been married for eleven years, you must have stopped having sex ten-and-a-half years ago. Nothing could be further from the truth. At least for Brenda and me, it's just gotten better.

Others are surprised when I joke about wanting sex with my wife, because they think Christians aren't supposed to talk about that. But God did. In fact, one whole book of the Bible, Song of Solomon, is all about sex. It is so descriptive. Read it sometime, and you'll see what I am referring to.

So we talk about sex. A lot. In fact, Brenda is always asking people, "How much sex do you have?" Apparently, she read somewhere that three times a week is average. This is the only area in Brenda's life where she's satisfied with being average. But this is another area where I'd like to improve my stats.

One time, Brenda got frustrated with me about how much was enough, so she asked, "What are you saying? One a day?"

"One a day plus vitamins," I teased her.

Sure, there are times in every marriage when you're busy with the kids and you're both tired. We have those struggles too. But I think many people are surprised at how much fun an old married couple can have. It's like a lifelong pass to the amusement park—you don't have to plan a vacation around it; you can take a ride anytime you want.

I love having sex with my wife because I love her. I know some of my teammates love having sex simply because they enjoy sex. While, obviously, I enjoy that too, there's so much more they'll never understand. All they know is the physical attraction, and they get bored after two days and start looking for someone else. For me, it's exactly the opposite. Every time I'm with my wife, it makes me want her more, not less.

When you really love somebody, that love goes beyond the physical. Yes, the physical is part of it, but it's only one facet. Everyone has days when they're not at their best. But when you love your wife, it's what you know about her that makes her so attractive to you. After all these years, I still enjoy Brenda. I enjoy observing her quirkiness, laughing together, and having great conversations—those things add to her beauty. That's something the single guys miss out on.

Time doesn't take those feelings away—it only intensifies them. Brenda will tell you there are still times when I walk by her and give her a little pat on the butt or touch her here or there. Often, those aren't the times most people would expect, like when she's all dolled up to go out. Instead, it's usually when she's wearing an apron and cooking for our kids or when she's wearing granny pajamas. I know she doesn't feel particularly sexy at those times, but those are the moments when I get a glimpse of who she is. And to me, it's like, *Wow. She's really sexy.*

"You're such a freak," she'll say, because she's always

surprised that at the time she feels least attractive, I find her most beautiful. But I like that. I don't think that's something my single friends get to enjoy.

In those moments, I grab her and kiss her passionately, not only for my own pleasure but also for the kids to see. Brenda's parents showed each other a lot of physical affection. Her mom would sit on her dad's lap to watch television. They were always touching each other and kissing in front of Brenda and even in front of Brenda's friends. We often talk about how they must have died holding hands when the tornado struck, because they were that close.

I want my kids to see that same kind of closeness. Because they range from ages three to nineteen, each one has a different reaction. Some just roll their eyes; others will say something like, "Oh, yuck; that's so gross!" When we watch TV, Brenda and I usually sit next to each other and cuddle. Often, there's a child in our laps too, but we're still together. And no matter what the kids say, I'm going to keep doing that because I want them to see how much I love their momma.

Premarital Sex

The first time I kissed Brenda was the night I met her. I kissed her on the cheek when I walked her to the car. But even after we officially started dating, we took things pretty slow. She was guarded because of her past, and I wasn't the kind of guy who was just interested in a quick twenty minutes. I wanted something more meaningful, and Brenda offered that.

But we did start sleeping together while we were dating.

The Bible has some pretty clear standards regarding sex out-side of marriage, but at the time I wasn't a believer. I think Brenda would say that because she'd already been married, it didn't matter that much to her. But after I put Jesus first in my life, I read the Bible more and found the sections that talked about sex being reserved for marriage.

Though Brenda taught me a lot about the Bible and encouraged me to read many passages—those weren't the ones she wanted to me to find. When I first talked to her about what I'd read, she said, "Are you kidding me? You found that? Out of all the things you could find in the Bible, you found 'no premarital sex'?"

But from the time I made a commitment to Christ, I always tried to do what the Bible said. So even though we had slept together for years while we were dating, we stopped hav-ing sex about a year before we got married. Did we fail a few times? Yes, we did. But we both really believed that the Bible had wisdom in this area, and we did our best to follow its advice.

Now it has come full circle as we've had to have conversa-tions with our seventeen-year-old daughter, Jesse, about what the Bible teaches and our expectations for her. Brenda and I have been open and honest with her. She knows we lived together and had sex before we were married, but she also knows we want something better for her.

Brenda has already told you about the away games when she takes each kid with her for some special one-on-one time. Last year, Brenda took Jesse for an away game around the time of her sixteenth birthday. Brenda brought along a purity ring for me to give to Jesse during our dinner together on Saturday night. Over dinner, we talked about some deep stuff. We told her how we wanted her to wait for someone who was as good as she deserved. We talked about how we didn't want her to lose the joy of her future by becoming so involved with a boyfriend that instead of enjoying college, she spent her time missing him. Most of all, we talked about waiting for the right time.

"We want you to be committed to this, and we're here for you; as a symbol of our dedication, we got you this." I gave her the purity ring.

She started crying.

Then I started crying.

Brenda the Marine never cries.

As Jesse put the ring on her finger, I said, "Don't let twenty minutes of fun ruin your life."

Then Brenda laughed. Not just a chuckle—an all-out, belly-shaking laugh.

"What's so funny?" I asked.

"Why did you put a time frame on it? Like, who says it's twenty minutes? It might be ten for them, or for some people it might last an hour. Did you ever think of that?"

So we had this deep moment, and Brenda laughed her head off. She kept repeating, "Don't let twenty minutes of fun ruin the rest of your life."

Soon, all three of us were laughing. Although I think Jesse understood what I tried to say, I think she also learned that sex wasn't a taboo topic. We could talk about it without getting all weird.

{ BRENDA }

Larry Fitzgerald once jokingly said to Kurt, "Being married is like eating spaghetti every night for the rest of your life."

I can't tell you how mad his little joke made me. Here's a guy who views our lifelong commitment as a plate of pasta. Larry's comment disturbed me not only because I don't look at marriage that way but also because I know Kurt doesn't like pasta. Kurt's more a meat and potatoes man, and Larry knew that, too.

On the other hand, I have to admit there's comfort in knowing you're going to have something to eat every night. You never have to go looking for food—or worse, go hungry.

But I think Larry has it all wrong. Not that I can blame him; he's not married. But marriage is not like spaghetti; it's more like a buffet that's always there for you to pick and choose what you want, depending on your appetite. There are just some things single guys won't understand until they're married.

A few weeks after Larry made that comment, we saw him at a black-tie event. Kurt and I got there late, which is really unusual for us.

"There you are! Where have you been?" Larry asked

When he kissed me on the cheek, I whispered in his ear, "We're late because Kurt and I had a quickie in the elevator."

To this day, Larry doesn't know whether that's true. And Kurt and I aren't telling him.

Let's just say we like our buffet kept fresh. That's why I send Kurt flirty text messages during the day. If someone else gets ahold of his phone, we're both in trouble; but I like knowing that I make him smile when he's away.

Sometimes when he is traveling out of town, I'll hide one of my nighties in his suitcase. I hope when he unpacks it he thinks, *I remember when she wore this.*

I always put love notes into his playbook when he leaves for an away game. He's never mentioned them, but I know he reads them and I know they will embarrass him, in a good way, so it makes me smile too.

Although there are things I do to deliberately keep the flame burning, sometimes it's the things I least expect that excite him. It's hot in Phoenix, so I wear a lot of sundresses. When he sees me in one, he'll say, "Wear that to bed tonight." It's happened so often that when I show up in a sundress to go shopping with my girlfriends, they'll tease me and say, "Why are you wearing lingerie?" But at least sundresses are a lot more comfortable than the lace and snap thingamajigs their husbands want them to wear.

But I don't need to be in a sundress for Kurt to get excited. The other night, I wasn't feeling well, so I went upstairs to change into a plaid flannel-like shirt with snaps down the front and matching pajama pants. The jammies were a gift from Betsy, our nanny, after a conversation about how some-times women just want to be comfortable. I found my favorite pink fuzzy slippers and pulled my hair back into a ponytail. I hadn't showered, and I wasn't wearing any makeup. Not exactly how you'd prepare for a night of hot action.

I went downstairs to make dinner, and while I was cook-ing, I splattered spaghetti sauce across my chest—because you know that's where it hits every time. I tried to clean up, but Kurt kept coming by and grabbing me. I thought about asking him to stop, but I just didn't want to fight it. And obviously he was having fun, because he kept doing it.

After dinner, we were busy cleaning up the kitchen and the kids were off doing their thing when he grabbed me and pulled me into the pantry. He wanted to make out. I'm thinking, *Dude, I am so not wanting this right now. That's why I put on the flannel jammies—to give you the signal.* But it didn't matter what I was thinking because he just kept going. Fortunately, he had to stop kissing me because one of the kids came back into the kitchen and needed something.

But later, after we went to bed, things heated up again.

We have one of those beds that is separated down the middle so that each person can raise or lower his or her own side. I've had a bad back for years (probably from carrying seven babies), and although it creates a Grand Canyon split in the middle of our bed, the separate controls really help me.

So later that night, after the pantry incident, I'm lying flat on my back on my side of the bed. I have my legs and feet elevated like I do when my back hurts. I'm thinking that's a clear signal that I'm not in the mood. But like most men, Kurt either doesn't notice or he doesn't care. He came into the room, turned off the TV, and then gave me the look.

You know the look I'm talking about.

"So?" he says.

"Seriously? You've got to be kidding me!"

He laughed. "What? I just want you."

"What do you want?" I asked, as if I didn't know.

"I just find you so attractive."

I gave every negative signal I could possibly give.

183

That I didn't feel attractive.

That I wasn't in the mood.

And that I didn't want it then.

But despite all that, when I saw how interested in me he was, something inside of me switched on, and I was interested too. I think because he found me so attractive, it made me feel attractive.

As Kurt mentioned, at moments like that, I call him a freak because it feels so weird that he would want me when I don't even want myself. But if it does it for him, then it does it for me.

Being Creative

Of course, when you have seven kids, finding moments alone can be tricky. We recently put a lock on our door to keep the younger kids from just walking in. Our room is our sanctuary.

In some ways, I'm trying to teach Jesse what a bedroom sanctuary means. For example, I don't think there's a reason for a boy to go into her room—ever.

I don't care how many of her friends do it. I don't care who the boy is. I don't care if he's just a friend. I don't care if he's gay. I want her bedroom to be extra special. I don't want a boy sitting on the bed where she sleeps at night. Her room is her private place. Although it may not be a big deal for some of her friends, I want Jesse to understand that until she gets married, her bedroom is her sanctuary, and then it will be a sanctuary for her and her husband.

I hope she grows up to cherish her room as much as we cherish ours. I try to model that for the kids by teaching them that our bedroom is our private place, not a place where they can barge in anytime. The marriage bed is also a sacred space and should be protected. The big kids get it; the little ones still forget to knock. That's why we put a lock on our door.

During the off-season, when Kurt and I are both home and our nanny is watching the kids, we'll say, "Betsy, we're really tired. We're going to go upstairs and take a nap."

She'll just grin. "Got it."

Sometimes on date night, we'll text Betsy that we're coming home early and that we're going to sneak in the front door and head upstairs. She'll keep the kids corralled, so they don't even realize we're home.

We also have a small guest casita that isn't attached to the house. Once we had enough kids to fill the bedrooms, we built the casita for our family and friends to stay in when they visit. Occasionally, Kurt and I sneak out there. No one knows where we are or what we're doing. It's funny to think we used to sneak around so my parents wouldn't catch us; now we sneak around so our kids don't catch us.

Kurt and I have fun together, and we try to keep things fresh. One of the reasons we still want each other so much is because we allow opportunities to miss each other. We give ourselves permission to go away. Just like we're better parents when we have time away from the kids, we're better partners when we've had a little time away from each other.

I probably get more weekends away with my friends than Kurt gets with his, but I don't have to feel guilty about taking a girls' weekend. No one keeps score. We have the freedom to do what we want because we both know that time away can be a good thing. Parting isn't sweet sorrow; parting is good for the marriage—and for our sex life.

Kurt would say that being apart makes us cherish each other more than we would otherwise. We don't get sick and tired of each other because we allow our partner to experience new things and bring them back to the marriage. For example, I'm currently studying photography, and I love coming home after a lesson and taking pictures of Kurt—although I'm not sure he always likes being my model.

There are times when I am looking at him through the lens of my camera, and I think, *I get to sleep and wake up next to this man for the rest of my life.* Maybe that means more to me that it does to other people. Coming from a broken marriage and then losing my parents, I appreciate the people who are in my life every day. And I look at Kurt and think, *I get him.*

Kurt is beautiful from the moment he wakes up, and he becomes more beautiful throughout the day because of what he does and who he is. What's more, I know that in thirty years he's going to be even more beautiful. I feel like I won a prize without having to compete for it. I'll gladly take that spaghetti dinner every night for the rest of my life.

fight fair

{ KURT }

It was date night, and Brenda was telling me a funny story. As I took a bite of my sandwich, she told me the punch line, expecting a big laugh. Just then, over my right shoulder, I heard, "I'm sorry to bother you, but would you sign this for me?" Before I could swallow, a kid slid a napkin in front of me and placed a pen in my hand.

I knew what Brenda was thinking. *Don't do it. Don't do it.* But I did it anyway. "Here you go."

"Thanks, Mr. Warner!"

As I reached for my sandwich, she said, "I'd go wash your hands. That kid sounded like he had a cold."

On my way to the washroom, three more people stopped me. By the time I got back to the table, I couldn't remember what Brenda was talking about, so I changed the subject and asked how her day had been. As she answered, I picked up my sandwich to take a bite. This time, the voice came from over my left shoulder.

"Mr. Warner, my son Bobby is your biggest fan." Bobby was clutching his dad like I was a three-headed monster. There was no way Bobby wanted to talk to me. "Could you sign this for Bobby? Just make it out to Robert—that's his full name."

After I finished signing Bobby's (or Robert's) torn envelope, a middle-aged woman approached. "Sorry to interrupt, but . . ."

I can't count how many date nights have started out exactly like that and ended in a fight on the way home.

"It's my night, and I can't even have a conversation with you," Brenda would complain.

"I can't help it," I'd argue. "I didn't ask them to come up."

"Well, you could have told them that you were with your wife and you weren't going to sign anything."

"If I had to explain to everyone why I wouldn't sign, that would have taken longer. If you don't want them bothering you, the fastest way to get it over with is to sign."

And on and on the fight would go.

I don't know about you, but I hate to fight. I hate being at odds with my wife, and I just want to fix things and make them right. But as much as I love Brenda, there are some things I just can't give in on. One is signing autographs when people ask me.

All the fan wants is a small piece of celebrity or maybe a signed football card from someone they think is a hero. They don't know how many people came to our table before they did, and they have no idea how many will come after. All they know is how I treated them.

It's likely that's the only personal encounter I will have
with those people. Either they'll think I was nice, or they'll
think I was a jerk. Their experience will shape their whole
view of me—and of Brenda, if she's with me. Whatever happens, they'll probably tell the story over and over again to
their friends and family.

I see each signing as an opportunity to earn their favor.
If I sign autographs for people and then they hear that I am
speaking at a local church, maybe they'll come hear what I
have to say. If I am talking in an interview, maybe they won't
switch the channel. Maybe because they once met me, they
will give my words a little more credence than they would
someone else's. Signing isn't a big deal to me, but sometime
down the road, it might make a difference to the person who
asked for my autograph.

How do I know? Because I get letters from people telling
me how much it meant to their son or daughter or husband
that I took the time to sign. Giving people a few seconds of
my time means I have an opportunity to influence their lives.

That's why I feel so strongly about it.

But over time, and after a lot of fights, I started to also
understand Brenda's frustration. It's not that I wanted to
choose strangers over my wife or kids, which is what Brenda
sometimes thought. That's not going to happen. If I were
given an ultimatum, I would choose my family, hands down.
But I also know that my family loves me and they're not going
to give me an ultimatum, because they know that signing
autographs is important to me. Even if I disappoint them at
the moment I choose to sign, when we leave the restaurant

and head home, they're going to get 100 percent of my attention.

So what do Brenda and I do when we're at odds about a subject like that? Like most couples, we fight. But if we're going to argue, one of our rules is that we argue from a place of love.

That means that, even when I am at my angriest, even when I am convinced my point is right and hers is wrong, I try to remember that my love for her is more important than anything we're arguing about. Doing so helps me to always hear what she has to say, to take action when I can, and to find ways to compromise. For example, with the autograph dilemma, here's how I approached the disagreement and what I did to try to resolve it.

First, I always try to listen to Brenda's concerns, and sometimes the concerns behind the ones she's expressing. With the signings, she wasn't so unreasonable that she expected me never to sign autographs; her real concern was trying to protect our family time.

Second, I take action on the things I can do something about. Though I wasn't going to stop signing autographs, I did promise that when I was at home, Brenda had 100 percent of my attention (unless, of course, I was "in the zone").

Finally, I look for ways to compromise. Now instead of date nights, we often do date afternoons. We can sneak into a matinee after the previews start and then take a side exit while the credits roll to avoid the crowds at the main entrance. We avoid crowded restaurants and instead frequent smaller restaurants where the owners know us. They help us maintain our privacy by seating us in the back or by running interference when other patrons want autographs.

Another thing we've done to protect our family time is to tell people to request autographs through the First Things First Foundation. That relieves our extended family of the pressure from people who are always asking them to get autographs from me, and it protects our time when we're together.

Though Brenda and I used to fight a lot about this issue, over time we've mostly worked through it. We both know where we stand, and we've agreed to disagree. But we've both also taken responsibility for contributing to a workable solution.

Pick Your Battles

If you read chapter 8, you already know that we occasionally fight about money. Seems like a silly thing for people who have so much to fight about, doesn't it? But as Brenda mentioned, what typically happens is that a friend or family member will ask me for money, and unless I clearly hear God tell me not to, I give it.

Brenda hates that, because she's seen how many of our relationships have changed because of money. When someone asks, she'll make a valid case for why I shouldn't give, and if her argument sways me, I'll change my mind. But often it doesn't, so I go ahead and give the money.

"So, your opinion is more important than mine?" she once asked.

"In my mind, it is," I said. Then I realized how that

sounded, so I quickly added, "Just as, in your mind, your opinion is more important."

That didn't help.

"I don't want to make you mad," I said, though I was dangerously close, "but I believe what I believe. To me, that's going to be more important to me than whatever it is you believe. And you're the same way."

In every marriage, there comes a time when one spouse's opinion is set in stone. No matter what the other person does, the belief can't be changed. When Brenda and I get to that point, I stop and ask myself, "Do I really feel strongly about this position, or am I just trying to win a fight?"

I am very competitive, so I admit that sometimes I just want to win. During those moments, I have to reexamine my behavior. But this time, I felt very strongly about the money issue, so Brenda backed down. We've had other arguments where she felt strongly and I've backed down. Brenda tells our kids to pick their battles. And that's one of the rules when we fight. We have to pick the hills we're willing to die on; on the other hills, we need to retreat.

Sometimes when we fight, my instincts are not very mature. Recently, for example, a woman I didn't know well gave me a hug, and I hugged her back. Later, Brenda was upset that I had "hugged a stranger." She started a fight over it, and I couldn't believe it.

At those moments, I want to keep score. I want to say to her, "But I saw you hug that dude that you just met, so what's the difference?" It's like a little devil on my shoulder telling me, "Say this. Tell her. Remind her of when she did it."

But I never say it—because it doesn't get us anywhere.

What good would it do if I pointed out her actions? Would it make her any less mad? Would she turn to me and say, "Oh, I forgot. It's okay for you to hug that woman now"?

No. She is still going to feel what she feels.

Sometimes it feels as if we make up our own rules as we go along, so I'm never sure what's going to make Brenda mad. But just when I am most frustrated with her, she'll say, "You don't know what it feels like to be cheated on when you're pregnant."

And there's no question about that; I don't. In those moments, I see that her pain comes from something far deeper than what I just did.

That's why another rule is that we don't keep score when we fight. Whoever she hugged or I hugged, that's in the past, and it isn't going to change the feelings that we're experiencing in the present. Keeping score doesn't settle an argument; it just prolongs it.

Understanding the pain that fuels her anger stops the fight. So instead of pushing for my own advantage, I try to really focus on, and hear, what Brenda's saying. Even if I don't know what I did wrong, I want to know what I can do to keep her from reliving that pain again.

If Brenda and I could struggle through the Hy-Vee days, when she was putting herself through school and we had two kids, what situation can we not make it through today? Are we really going to let fights over autographs, money, or hugging a stranger tear us apart?

Even when we fight, I still love Brenda. If she knows that

I love her, then I think it's harder for her to stay mad at me. If she knows how I really feel, she can't just get angry and say I'm a horrible husband. She has to think, *Even though he hugged that woman, he still loves me. Is it worth it to keep fighting?*

I don't know what we could fight about that would be big enough to change the overall picture of how much I love and care for Brenda. She's my wife, and I wouldn't want to live with anybody else.

{ BRENDA }

I was trained to be a Marine. That means I know how to fight, and I know how to protect. And when I fight, it's usually because I'm trying to protect something. I am confident in my ability to support my argument, and I am passionate when I make my case. I like that. I like that my kids see that. I am not a pushover, and I don't want my kids to be dominated by their future spouses, either.

This past year, I took Kade to the Seattle away game. True to form, he played his Nintendo DS and didn't pay a bit of attention to the game. The Cardinals were ahead of the Seahawks, and I was screaming like a madwoman. I already have a loud voice, and I can applaud rather enthusiastically, so I was probably annoying the Seahawks fans in my section.

The woman in front of me got very irritated, and when she couldn't stand the cheering any longer, she turned around and said, "If you don't shut up, I'm going to choke you with your red scarf."

I looked at Kade to see if he had heard what she said. He

looked up at me, glanced at the lady, and before he looked back down at his DS, he said, "You can take her, Mom."

At ten years old, even my son was confident I could win a chick fight at a stadium. That's not exactly the lesson I wanted him to learn, but he was right. I could have taken her. And if I ever had to, I would. I'm the friend you want in your foxhole. You could trust me with your life. I am also that kind of wife and mother. There isn't anything I wouldn't do to fight for my family.

When Kurt and I fight, it is usually about one of the three subjects he mentioned: autographs, money, or other women. Each issue is a hot button for me, but for different reasons.

I'm never mad about Kurt signing autographs at the stadium. That's his job, and that's the appropriate place to do it. But when it happens during our private time, or when it distracts him from his kids, that's when it upsets me.

Last week, Kurt was at Jada's softball game and could stay for only a few minutes because he wanted to get to Jesse's music performance. He got to the game late and joined us on the metal bleachers. As soon as he did, the kids were all over him. He had to unwrap Tootsie Pops, answer Elijah's questions, and keep an eye on Jada, who was up to bat—all at the same time.

Then a dad from the other team came over with his young son and asked Kurt for an autograph. Kurt signed it while trying to keep one eye on Jada, who had just hit the ball. Over the next few minutes, several more people came over—a couple of giggly preteen girls who wanted him to sign someone else's business card; a young man in his twenties, who had

Kurt sign a dollar bill for him and a softball for his brother; and a guy with a couple of dogs that scared my kids. No one acted rude or obnoxious; they were all very polite. I know they just wanted Kurt's autograph. But as a mother, it broke my heart to see that they always seemed to ask when Jada was up to bat or making a play at second base. She would turn to see if her dad had noticed, and instead, she would see him signing something for a stranger.

So when I fight with Kurt, I'm not against him being a good guy or a positive role model; I'm simply fighting for my kids, who want their dad to notice them. And I know that's also what Kurt wants. That's why he was at the game. That's also why he left early, so he could support Jesse and her music.

When Kurt and I argue, it's not that I want to win; it's that I want to be heard. Even if Kurt ultimately decides to do something other than what I want, I want to be respected for my views. I understand that I'm not going to win every fight; I don't need to or want to. But I do expect that he'll understand me and my position better than he did before the fight.

I have never viewed marital arguments as an opportunity to win or lose. My parents fought a lot when I was growing up—mostly over money and bills. We owned a pickup truck, and all four of us would sit in the front. When Mom was mad at Dad, she'd say something like, "Tell your father . . ."

And then Kim and I would say, "Dad, Mom said . . ."

But somehow we'd always mess up whatever it was we were supposed to pass on. It was a like a bad game of telephone, and every time it happened, my folks would soften up, and one of them would laugh.

So I knew from a young age that you could fight, make your position known, and continue to love your partner as if nothing had ever happened.

Rules for Fighting Fair
I am passionate; that's how God made me to be. So whether I am happy or angry, I'm going to express how I feel about a topic. But when it comes to fighting, I am careful that my passion is never directed at Kurt, only at the topic. For both of us, fighting is never about hurting each other or making the other person feel like he or she is less; it's only about making sure that we hear each other's point. We have a few rules that we follow to make sure we're fighting fairly:

1. We never fight dirty. Our fighting is all about getting our point of view across to the other person. The reason it's a fight instead of a discussion is because one or both of us is really passionate about the issue and the other person is in opposition. To resolve the conflict, we try to understand the other person's view and determine who cares most about the issue. We take turns giving our side of the argument. Kurt is very even-keeled. He doesn't holler back at me, and we don't interrupt each other or shut down—although there are certainly times when I want to go pout. Instead, we keep at it, expressing our opinions until the air clears.

2. We don't call each other names. No matter how off-base we think the other person's position is, we never resort to calling the other person stupid, or worse. We never make the argument about the other person—no matter how heated we are about the topic.

3. We fight in the moment. We don't bring up past behavior or pull a line like "Last time you . . . ." We fight only about the issue in front of us, and we try not to let it morph into something else.

4. We fight to be heard. Our fights are about opposing ideas, and our goal is to find a way to work through them.

5. We never lose sight of the big picture. We know that whatever we're fighting about isn't a deal breaker, so really, do we want to keep going or just get it over with?

6. There are no winners and losers. As we said, it's never about power, only about issues and ideas.

7. When it's done, it's done. We never mention it again unless it's to laugh about it.

Now I have to mention the one rule that supersedes the others. Kurt and I believe that you can ignore any of the rules if you're trying to make your partner laugh—as long as it's not at his or her expense.

The last time Kurt and I were in a heated argument, for

example, I jokingly swore by calling him a name to break the tension.

"Stop that," he said. And I knew I had him, because Kurt doesn't curse.

By now, I had the giggles, and he knew what was coming. There's a sports show on Fox that Kurt won't say the title of, and it always makes me laugh. "Say, '*The Best Damn Sports Show Ever*.'"

"I don't have to," he said, smirking. "I can call it the *Best Darn Sports Show* if I want."

With that, the argument was over. Neither of us could continue to make serious points when we were both laughing.

CHAPTER 14

nothing but the best for my wife

{ KURT }

On the Saturday night before a home game, our team checks into a local hotel. It's a way for us to keep free of distractions and focus on the game ahead.

But Brenda will tell you that I check out at home long before I check into the hotel.

When I get focused while I'm still at home, Brenda calls it "the zone," which is a polite way of saying what she's really thinking—that I'm crabby. She'll tell you there are times I'm in the zone long before Saturday. She knows I'm there because I'm short with her and the kids, I don't answer her questions with full sentences, and though I think my wife is one of the funniest people I know, I no longer laugh at her jokes.

When I enter the zone, all I can think about is the game. My mind is focused on what I have to do and how I'm going to do it. This past year, with the playoffs, I went into the zone even earlier than usual. One week, Brenda said I was gone as early as Tuesday.

201

Brenda and Jesse laugh at me because I can be working on the computer or going through plays, and they can yell or scream, and I don't listen. Sure, I hear their voices, and when forced to, I can even repeat verbatim what they said. But it doesn't register. They'll tell me they're heading out to the store, but when they get back, I'll say, "Did you go somewhere?" I don't realize they've already left and returned.

When I first started playing football, I was very bad about getting lost in my own thoughts. For some games, I was in the zone all week. The night before a game, Brenda would want to get together for dinner, but I would tell her no. I didn't want to be around anyone; I just wanted to be by myself. I've gotten better over the years. Now on Saturday nights before an away game, I eat dinner with Brenda and whichever one of the kids is along on the trip, and I'm a little more conversational than I used to be.

To me, "being in the zone" is just another way of saying I'm focused. Just as repetitive noises and the chaos of seven kids doesn't bother me while I'm reading a book, when I am preparing for a game, I am so focused that I can't think of anything else.

That intense focus especially happens on the field. While playing, I lose perspective on the overall game because I am so locked in to what I'm going to do next. Only after it's over do I consider the game in its entirety. That's when I can reflect on the lows and the highs—like the interception right before halftime or the touchdown that almost won the game for us.

I believe the ability to focus is one of my best qualities; it helps me stay cool in the pocket and complete a pass while being blitzed. But I can see how much it annoys my family, because it annoys me when my son does it. Kade has that same type of focus. While watching a movie, he's so locked in that he doesn't hear what's happening around him.

"Kade, you need to take out the trash," I'll tell him. Five minutes later, I look over expecting it to be done and it's not.

"Kade!" I'll yell. "What about the trash?"

He'll look at me like I'm crazy for yelling at him—but he never heard me the first time.

There are times when I'm proud of Kade's ability to shut out distractions. I hope it will contribute to his future success like it's helped me. On the other hand, I get a taste of Brenda's perspective when I try to get his attention and have to yell, "Hey, Kade! Will you listen to me?"

That's one of the reasons I try to be intentional about giving Brenda my attention when I'm not in the zone. It's so easy in our busy household to cross paths and not really talk or listen to each other. We shout directions for Jada's game, or instructions to pass on to the nanny, and we keep going, without ever slowing down to look each other in the eye and hear what the other has to say.

Fortunately, very early in our marriage, a friend encouraged Brenda and me to always make time for each other. With my career, there is so much that takes us away from home and family—whether it's the busyness of the season or the opportunities God gives us in the off-season—that when we're home, it's tempting just to spend our time with the kids and neglect each other.

I've discovered that I am a better parent if I have a break

from our children. And I'm a better husband when Brenda and I take a break together. So for years we've made it a priority to have a date night once a week. It's not easy; there are some weeks we'd both rather just stay home. But we are committed to making sure we get time alone.

The kids will be with us for about twenty years, but Brenda and I plan to be together forever. When we look at it that way, we realize that we need to prioritize *our* relationship. So Brenda pulls out her calendar, and we write in our date nights alongside doctor appointments and softball games. At the same time, we also schedule the nanny or a babysitter, because we don't want an excuse to cancel our plans at the last minute.

Occasionally, when I talk about date night, people will say to me that they don't have the money that we do, so going out each week isn't an option for them. I know it seems like a lot of money for a regular night out, but the flip side is, how much is it worth to have your wife know she's the center of your world? For families that can't afford to hire a sitter once a week, I would still encourage them to find a way to put the kids to bed, turn off the TV, and have a candlelit dinner on the deck or in their bedroom.

It's not about how much money we spend on date night. It's not about the food we eat or the movie we see—sometimes we even leave the movie early to have a conversation in the car. Rather, it's about the time we spend laughing together and talking to each other without the interruptions that happen at home.

In addition to our weekly date night, Brenda and I also

take two or three vacations each year without the kids. Sometimes we're only gone for two or three days; sometimes it's just a night at a local hotel; but it's private time for us to enjoy each other as people, not just as Mom and Dad. The key is that both our date nights and the vacations are intentional, planned activities. We don't just assume they'll happen spontaneously; we make them a priority.

Sometimes it's hard to leave the kids when we go on a vacation. But I also want them to know that my wife takes priority—even over them. There are not many things I would choose over my kids, so when I choose to spend time with Brenda—whether it's a date night, a vacation away, or just going to our bedroom to close the door so we can talk—I'm teaching my kids that she comes first. I want them to know that's what a marriage looks like. That's what it means to love someone—it means to choose that person first over and over again. I want my boys to see that so they will do the same thing when they're married. I want my girls to see that so they'll expect to be their husband's first priority when they get married.

During our time together, I do my best to make sure that I am completely focused on Brenda and that I'm listening—and hearing—what she has to say. Those are my opportunities to really understand her—who she is, what she wants, and what she needs from me. Sometimes it's as simple as sharing a few laughs; other times I hear about her dreams of being a photographer. But in those moments, I want her to know that I am doing my best to understand her.

I don't always get it right, as she'll tell you. But I try. One of the ways I try is by surprising her with gifts that show I understand her. For example, at some point after her parents died, she went through a stage in her grief where she'd suddenly realize she hadn't thought of her parents at all that day. And with that realization came guilt. Then, instead of a day, it was a week when she wouldn't think about them. And her feelings of guilt would intensify. We talked about it on several occasions, and I knew how much it bothered her. So I took a photo of her parents to a local artist, who hand-painted a picture of her mom and dad. Brenda will tell you that was one of her favorite gifts. It showed her that I understood what she was going through and that I wanted to support her in her grief.

I've also tried to show her understanding by allowing her to have time away from the kids and me—time to spend with her girlfriends. Although I don't need as much guy time myself, I know my wife needs to hang out with her friends occasionally, and I encourage her to do that—whether it's going away for a few days or just having a night out on the town.

For her fortieth birthday, Brenda and I flew to New York on a Thursday. We spent the night in a hotel and then did some shopping on Friday. That night, I took her to a special restaurant for her birthday dinner. "Reservations for two, Warner," I told the host when we walked in. He led us downstairs, where Brenda thought I had arranged a secluded table so we wouldn't be bothered. Instead, she found six of her closest girlfriends seated around a large table.

Her friends were from different periods in her life, and

they lived in different parts of the country. Some had not met each other before. I had arranged for them to come to New York and meet Brenda at the restaurant. I left them alone and flew out the next morning so she could have the next two days with her friends.

I realize that sounds like an expensive luxury that many people can't afford, but my point isn't the cost. The point of that weekend was that I invested time and energy in planning it. I didn't give Brenda's birthday just glancing attention; I took the time to plan the things I knew she would want most on that birthday—spending time with her girlfriends.

Brenda has lots of layers, and it has taken time and attention throughout the years to get to know all of her. I haven't always planned the best birthdays. Sometimes I missed the mark because I didn't take her needs into account. But by making an effort to understand her, I've learned a lot.

One thing I've realized is that it doesn't take an expensive weekend in New York to show Brenda that I love her. I could probably have done the same thing at a local restaurant—by simply surprising her with dinner with some friends. In fact, Brenda's favorite memories from the New York trip didn't cost a thing. The one she talks about most is when everyone went around the table and said what they loved most about her. You may remember that's one of the rules we talked about in chapter 4; we always do that at the dinner table when someone is having a birthday. Well, the rule applied to Brenda's dinner with friends as well. For Brenda, hearing her girlfriends express their love for her was a memorable moment.

{ BRENDA }

My fortieth birthday was very special. In fact, I sometimes consider it a makeup birthday for the one Kurt blew in my midthirties. "Only the best for my wife," he jokes, and I have to say, he did try to do the "best" part. Unfortunately, he forgot about the "for my wife" part.

We were living in St. Louis at the time, and it was after Kurt had signed the big contract, so we could afford to do what we wanted. Luxuries were still new to us, and at that time in our lives, he knew I was enjoying a few perks of his fame. On this particular day, I was in the kitchen, talking to a girlfriend, when Kurt came in and said, "Pack a nice outfit, a casual outfit, and put on your swimsuit."

Though I hate surprises, at first I was excited. He had not only planned a trip, but he had also thought ahead enough to arrange to have my girlfriend there as a babysitter. On the other hand, I wasn't very happy about wearing a bathing suit. What woman wants to put on her swimsuit and then go out?

I got dressed, we got in the car, and Kurt started driving. It was a long drive—something like an hour and a half. I noticed that Kurt was taking a lot of back roads, and I thought it was because he didn't want me to know where we were going. The problem was, I don't do road trips well. I get carsick. Kurt knew that, and I knew he knew that, so I thought where we were headed must be really special. I trusted him; he obviously had it all planned out. So, for an hour and a half we were on back roads, country highways, and country roads. I was sitting in the passenger seat of the car in my swimsuit, and my thighs were starting to rub. I hoped it wasn't the beginning of a rash. The scene wasn't pretty, but I knew Kurt had something spectacular planned.

Finally, he turned down a road that led into a park, and a beautiful lake opened up before us. I saw a guy with two jet skis waiting for us. We climbed on the jet skis and took off. Kurt wanted to race, because everything's a competition to him, so we raced. I don't need to tell you who won. After a couple hours of this, we returned the skis and got back in the car. I was still in my swimsuit, and now I was also wet. My hair had been blowing in the wind, and I had gotten a little sun on my face. In short, I was not at my most attractive, so I was hoping we were not going anywhere where I would be seen in public. At that time in St. Louis, the press loved to take pictures of me with Kurt and make comments like, "She looks like his mother," or "Why would a Christian woman get a Jewish nose job?" (I've never had a nose job.) Nice, huh?

Kurt drove a little farther, and we pulled into the historic town of Hannibal, Missouri, best known for being the hometown of Mark Twain. Kurt called it historic; I called it old.

Because Kurt was at the height of his celebrity, he didn't want people to know we were in town and where we were staying. We stopped at a bed-and-breakfast, but instead of using the main entrance, he ushered me through the back door. When Kurt and I walked through the door, I was expecting an entryway, but instead we were in a kitchen that was so tight we had to turn sideways to get through. And, of course, I was still in my swimsuit.

As we turned the corner and came out of the kitchen, we passed through an itty-bitty living room with plastic on the furniture and a nineteen-inch TV on top of one of those TV trays that people used to eat on in the 1950s. The TV had rabbit ears with tin foil stuck to the top.

This wasn't the kind of birthday surprise I was expecting. As we started up the stairs, I was thinking, *This is a joke. I'm being punk'd.* I started looking for the cameras.

When we opened the door to the bedroom, it looked like Flowers-R-Us had thrown up. There were floral patterns on the bedspread, curtains, doilies, wallpaper, towels, and carpet. And none of them matched. At this point, I still thought Kurt was joking, because there was no way that you could know me and think this is what I would want. Pick ten friends of mine and call them and ask what you should do for my birthday. They'd all say, "Don't take her to a bed-and-breakfast in Hannibal, Missouri!"

Kurt told me to get dressed in the nice outfit; we were going to the best restaurant in town. I was thinking, *Keep a good attitude. The real gift is still coming.*

I changed into a long, black skirt with a bustier on top. It was dramatic and sexy. I went all out. I wore my diamond earrings, high heels, and Spanx to pull in my belly. When I came out, Kurt said, "Wow!" which is what I like him to say when I go to all that trouble.

We went back downstairs, walked past the plastic furniture, squeezed through the kitchen, and got in the car. I looked good, and Kurt also looked great—he was all decked out too. The night was starting to look up. Although the accommodations weren't what I would have chosen, I was still looking forward to our big night out.

At that point, Kurt knew that the room wasn't what either one of us was expecting, so he wanted to make it up to me. He said, "I'm taking you to the best restaurant in town, LulaBelle's."

We pulled into the parking lot, and the first thing I saw was an older couple—they were like in their nineties—heading to the front door and wearing shorts and flip-flops! I'm thinking, *You've got to be kidding me!*

Kurt saw them too, and so he told me that he really didn't know anything about the restaurant. Someone else had recommended it. (He knew this wasn't going to be good, so he was trying to blame it on someone else!) Still trying to make the best of it and hoping there was a private dining room, we went in, and the hostess seated us in the main dining area. As I sat down, I realized that everyone else was staring at us. I looked like Dolly Parton, and they were all in flip-flops.

But I became even more embarrassed about my sexy wardrobe choice when I saw that the inside of the restaurant was decorated with pieces of lingerie. Turns out, LulaBelle's used to be a brothel. *Can this get any worse?* I hiked up my bustier.

We were the youngest people in the restaurant by, like, thirty years. Of course, we were also the most dressed up. I was so embarrassed that I couldn't even eat my food. Every time I looked down, I saw my chest and thought, *I got dressed up for this?* More than anything, I just wanted to disappear.

And I was livid at Kurt, thinking, *He* planned *this? He thought this was something I would like?*

It wasn't until later that I learned the accommodations had surprised him as much as they had me. He had relied on the recommendations of others rather than checking into them himself.

Just when I thought it couldn't get any worse, I heard singing and saw a parade of waiters and waitresses carrying a sheet cake toward our table. A sheet cake! The cake said, "Happy Birthday, Brenda," and the whole restaurant joined in the singing.

Later, Kurt told me he had ordered the cake ahead of time, and he'd had to pay an extra $10 to get them to write "Happy Birthday" and an extra $5 to get them to add "Brenda." He thought he was going all out. I thought that should have been a clue he was in the wrong place.

Finally, we paid the bill and left the restaurant. Once in the car, I yanked off my fake eyelashes and stuck them on the dash so they were looking at us the whole way back to the bed-and-breakfast. The rash from my swimsuit had worsened because of the Spanx rubbing against my thighs, and though I knew I shouldn't be angry with Kurt, I was so disappointed at the way the evening had turned out that I couldn't control my emotions.

We got back to the bed-and-breakfast and did the kitchen thing again, but this time when we passed the plastic furniture and the tinfoil TV, the couple who ran the place stopped us. "Would you like to join us for a little TV?" they offered. They and the couple next to them looked up at us expectantly.

To me, their questions seemed like all the proof I needed that Kurt either didn't understand me or didn't care. I thought it was the latter. He knew how uncomfortable I was making small talk with strangers. Now we were being asked to join strangers on the plastic couch for some television time? I let Kurt have the honor of answering their question.

Upstairs, I didn't want to get into the bed with the nasty floral sheets. To some people, the faded look might make them seem comfortable; to me, they just looked used. But at this point, Kurt and I were not speaking, so what else could I do? I got into bed.

All I could think was, *After all this time, how can he not know me better than this?*

Kurt knew he was in trouble, and he also knew he wasn't going to get anywhere with me that night. We were both stuck lying there with the lights on, no TV in our room, and nothing to do. Because I hadn't had much time to pack, I hadn't thought to grab a book; but after I crawled into bed, I found a journal on the nightstand—you know, the kind of book where people who've stayed in the room leave little notes to people who will stay there in the future? So I picked it up and started reading.

> *"We're on the way to my mother's funeral, and my husband thought that stopping here would cheer me up a little. . . ."*

> *"My wife and I have never had a vacation, but we were finally able to save up enough to stay here. . . ."*

The stories were so touching that I couldn't put the journal down.

*"We sat down to watch TV, and the people who run
the place joined us and they were the nicest people."*

Kurt had a journal on his side of the bed as well, and he
started reading his, too. People wrote about the wonder-
ful dinner they'd had at LulaBelle's and how much they had
enjoyed it. I started reading Kurt some of the stories in my
journal, and he read me some from his.

Kurt said, "I knew we were in trouble when I heard the
name of the restaurant was LulaBelle's."

"Then why didn't you cancel?"

"Because it was the best restaurant in Hannibal."

I started laughing—I couldn't help it. It was such a ridicu-
lous thing to say, even if it was true. And that broke the ice.
We laughed together about the old people in flip-flops, about
our getting so dressed up, about the plastic furniture and the
TV with the foil on the antenna. He told me how he had
paid extra to get my name on the sheet cake. And we laughed
about the room decor as we tried to see how many floral patterns we could count.

It was nothing I would ever choose to do again, and it certainly wasn't the Ritz, but by the time we went to sleep, we'd
had a good time just enjoying each other's company and sense
of humor.

The next morning, we ate a communal breakfast with the
other guests, the way you often do in a bed-and-breakfast.
It was way out of my comfort zone, but I did it to let Kurt
know that I appreciated his efforts—no matter how far short
they had fallen from the goal. Afterward, we got the heck out

of town. As we made the road trip home, I realized that he hadn't taken back roads to throw me off track—that was the only way to get to Hannibal.

Kurt immediately knew that the trip wasn't what I would have chosen. In fact, had he known, he wouldn't have chosen it either. But we both learned a few things on that trip. Kurt no longer relies on the recommendations of strangers who don't know us and our preferences. And just because something is "the best of" doesn't mean it's the best for us.

Kurt has worked hard to truly understand me. Even now, years later, when Kurt says, "Nothing but the best for my wife," it makes me laugh, because I know he gets it.

CHAPTER 15

use your words

{ KURT }

Sometimes the media portray me as some kind of perfect dad or perfect Christian. But that's not accurate. Like everyone else, I mess up every day. I get mad when I'm taking care of the kids and they won't take a nap when I want them to, or when we're playing a game and they're not playing the way I want them to play. Sometimes I resent having to watch them—even when I chose to do it in the first place.

Brenda has already mentioned that I'm the one who picks up the slack at our house. She's right. I do. There have been times when I've turned down ministry opportunities because I felt I needed to stay home and help with the kids. There are other times when what I really need is just to get alone with God for a while and try to sort through all the things I feel he's teaching me, but instead of telling Brenda, "I can't help you right now," or maybe calling the nanny, I still jump in and help with the kids.

But I don't always do it with the best attitude. Sometimes

I think, *Fine, I don't have time for this right now, but I'll just do it. Then everyone will see what a great dad I am.*

Of course, at that point, I'm not helping out Brenda for her sake or because I'm really focused on the kids. I'm giving in because there's a certain satisfaction sometimes in playing the martyr—and because I haven't bothered to tell Brenda that right now what I really need is time to take care of other things.

I've learned that the moments when I'm the most frustrated are not when I'm thinking about my wife or the kids but when I'm thinking about myself. When I step up and do what I'm asked to do but am angry the whole time, I've missed the target. I may *look* like the world's greatest dad, but I know I'm thinking only of myself. And God knows it too.

When I'm the biggest martyr, I'm also the biggest loser. That's not who I want to be. What I want to be is a dad who takes care of his kids because he's truly committed to them, not so that in the end I can say, "Hey, everybody thinks I'm a great dad because I worked so hard and sacrificed so much."

Because I don't work a nine-to-five job and I'm often home when other dads would be at work, it's easy for me to get sucked into thinking I have to spend every waking moment with my kids. But just because I'm home doesn't mean I have the day off. There are foundation responsibilities, preparing for ministry opportunities, and football-related "homework." So sometimes I need to take care of my business and personal responsibilities rather than pitching in with the kids.

Brenda and I have learned that when we make time for the things we need to do rather than try to squeeze them into the leftover minutes that never seem to be there, we are better parents. So if I focus on getting done what needs to be done, then my energy and attention can be fully focused on my kids when I'm with them, not on what I still need to do, and I won't be so quick to resent the fact that I said nothing, gave in, and helped out when I still had other things on my to-do list. That brings me to one of the most important rules in our house: If you want something, you have to ask for it.

You Have to Ask

Brenda touched on this rule in a previous chapter when she explained that the kids are responsible to ask for help with their homework if they need it. We live our lives by that rule; if you need something, it's your job to ask. You need to use words and not expect others to read your mind.

Sierra and Sienna are perfect examples. When they're frustrated, they'd rather scream, "Aaaah!" than use real words. But we don't want them yelling in frustration; we want them to tell us what's wrong. So we force them to use words to communicate, even when they don't want to.

The other day, Sierra screamed as she struggled to get her sleeves pulled out of her sweater.

"I don't know what you want until you tell me," Brenda said. "You have to use your words to communicate."

Of course, Brenda knew what Sierra wanted. But she made Sierra talk about it before she would help her out.

She didn't do that to be mean; she did it because we know that for the rest of Sierra's life, she will have to use words to communicate. She'll need to use words to tell another person what she wants and what she needs—whether that person is her boss at work, her boyfriend, or even God.

I know a lot of women struggle with telling their husbands what they want. They hold back expressing their needs when it comes to doing the housework, needing help with the kids, or getting what they want in the bedroom. I'm fortunate that Brenda doesn't struggle in this area at all. She clearly communicates her needs and desires. Some of them are serious, and some are silly, but they're all clearly communicated.

For example, as Brenda already mentioned, she grew up thinking she was "the pretty one" in her house. Her time in the Marines reinforced that idea, because there were so few women in the Corps and Brenda is very attractive. But when her first husband cheated on her, it left her with lots of doubts. Maybe she wasn't pretty enough.

After the Rams won the Super Bowl, there was a lot of media attention given to how Brenda looked—especially the clothes she wore and her short, spiky hairstyle (which I loved). Her doubts really caught fire when she read magazine and Internet accounts of herself. Each critical or negative article chipped away at her self-esteem. And though she knows I think she's the most beautiful woman in the world, she can't hear it enough.

So she'll say to me, "Tell me I'm beautiful." Or she'll say, "When I come downstairs after getting all dolled up, I want you to say, 'Wow!'"

Like Brenda, I want to be able to say what I need. And if I want things to change, I need to voice my desires. That's the rule at our house, and it's also the only way others know how to help meet our needs. Good communication solves problems. But it can also help us to identify problems.

We've already talked about some of the differences in our parenting styles. Here's another one. Growing up, I was spanked, and spanked a lot. But Brenda grew up in a house where she and her sister were never spanked. In fact, she rarely remembers being disciplined at all. So as we came together, we had to find the best way to discipline our kids. Often it meant that I spanked and she didn't.

One day, Elijah did something that the Babygirls didn't like. So Sienna went over to the drawer and got out the wooden spoon, like she'd seen me do so many times. I asked her what she was doing, and she said, "He's bad."

She was going to take the spoon and hit Elijah with it.

That's not the point I wanted my kids to take from my discipline—that when someone is bad you hit him or her with a wooden object. In that moment, Sienna clearly communicated to me that *I* wasn't clearly communicating to her when I used the spoon to discipline her and the other kids. Now we're trying to discipline more Brenda's way—with our words. And it seems to be working. If you asked Jada how we discipline, she'd say, "They punish us by talking to us." Though it sounds humorous, like the worst thing in the world we could do to punish her is to make her have a conversation with us, there is truth in her words. When it comes to disciplining, we do discuss things—a lot.

That works even with the youngest girls. For example, Sierra will come and say that Sienna took her doll. Together,

Sierra and I will walk over to Sienna, and I'll ask, "Sienna, did you take her doll?"

More often than not, Sienna will say no.

"Did you take the doll?" I'll ask again. "You need to tell me the truth. The complete truth."

That's when she breaks. "Yes, I took it."

At that point, I explain that Sierra needs the doll back, and I give Sienna the opportunity to make it right. She gets to choose. She knows what she did, and she knows how to fix it. I want to give her a chance to tell the truth, fix what she did, and not get into trouble for what she did. She gets to be the one who decides whether she gives the doll back or not. Usually, she does. But if not, the consequences will escalate to a time-out—or worse.

Throughout the disciplinary process, there is never a point at which the children think they can negotiate with me. They're the children, and I'm the parent, and they have to follow the rules. But as parents, Brenda and I want to give our kids the opportunity to self-discipline and choose to do what is right. We want them to know what's right and wrong and use their own words to communicate that to us and to each other. They need to learn how to use words to apologize and to ask for forgiveness.

So, Jada's right; we do "punish" them by talking. And though I wouldn't consider it punishment, there are times when we force the kids to do things they don't want to do. When Jesse was younger, she would get flustered when she had to leave a voice mail message. She would stutter and stammer and just couldn't make the words come out. She would be on the verge of tears and would try to hand Brenda or me the phone to do it for her, but we wouldn't do it. We forced her to do it for herself. I guess it worked, because Jesse can not only use her words to leave a message but also stand on stage and perform the words of famous playwrights without getting a bit flustered.

{ BRENDA }

Communication doesn't always fix the problem. Sometimes the kids don't give the dolls back, and sometimes husbands still break the rules.

As Kurt mentioned, one of our "supposed" rules is that he's not to sign autographs when he's with the kids. It's not a "supposed" rule; it is a rule. It's just one that he's not very good at keeping.

To understand my perspective, you have to know what a huge disruption it is when we're in public. The requests for Kurt to sign something or to pose for pictures are constant. *Constant.* After his first Super Bowl, we couldn't go anywhere without being overwhelmed by autograph requests. Eventually it died down, and by comparison, things have been pretty calm in Phoenix. But now, after another Super Bowl appearance, the circus has started all over again. Let me see if I can explain it.

You've probably had an experience where you were eating out with friends or family and an overzealous server kept interrupting your conversation.

"Does everything taste okay?"

"Do you need anything else?"

"Can I refill that for you?"

"Do you want dessert?"

You know he or she is just trying to be helpful, but when the conversation gets interrupted that many times, it's hard not to get a little annoyed.

Well, that's what it's like every time we go out to eat. Servers are overly attentive, and that's one thing, but fans constantly come up to the table to talk to Kurt—usually just after he's taken a bite of food. Then the manager comes over and introduces himself. After that, the chef comes out and says, "I hope you like my food."

But it doesn't just happen in restaurants. It happens at church, at the kids' school, and at the grocery store. Once, while I was home making supper, I sent Kurt to the store for a few items. On his way out of the store, a woman stopped him and asked if he'd sign something for her. Kurt said he would, but she couldn't find anything for him to write on; so instead she said, "My son has a poster hanging on his wall. I don't live far from here. Can you just follow me home and sign that?"

Of course, he didn't.

Personally, my favorite line—and Kurt hears it all the time—is, "I hate to interrupt, but if you could just sign this. . . ."

I think, *If you hate to interrupt, then why are you doing it?*

But Kurt just signs anyway.

I know that people are just interested in getting celebrity souvenirs, and it only takes a few seconds of Kurt's time to sign their items, but they don't realize how many requests have already come before and how many more will come after.

I understand why people do it, but I still don't like it; so it's one of those things that I continue to communicate my feelings about to Kurt. It's not that I don't love people; it's just that I hate autographs—and usually the two go together. I want Kurt to teach people that it's appropriate to ask for autographs at the stadium but it's not okay to ask for them while he's having dinner with his family. I want him to communicate that message so his fans will learn to be more aware and considerate, not only with us but also with other celebrities.

He, of course, would say that you can't teach everyone a lesson in ten seconds.

We argue—I mean *communicate*—about this topic a lot. But there are no good choices. Like Kurt said, it takes longer to explain the rule about not signing with the kids around than it does to just sign.

When it happens in restaurants, I sometimes make snarky comments that only Jesse can hear. Other times, I openly say something, such as, "Kurt, just finish your meal first." Sometimes that helps to remind people of their manners and they'll say, "Oh, sorry. I'll come back."

More often, I just choose to keep talking about it with Kurt. Though he may not change his position, I hope he'll at least understand mine. I'm trying to protect his time with his kids; every time he stops to sign an autograph, he takes his attention away from them. He never lets on that I'm right, but I can often tell he's thought about it and he realizes my feelings make some sense too. After eleven years of this, I need to pick another battle; I'm clearly not winning this one.

But it's through that process of communication that Kurt

sometimes takes a firmer stance with autograph seekers, and I learn to tolerate some things I otherwise wouldn't. Communication doesn't solve the issue for us completely. Kurt and I are always going to disagree on how to handle certain situations. But instead of keeping things bottled up inside and allowing bitterness to grow, we've learned to take what we can from the other person's view. We learn to make the best of our disagreement.

Whether or not we agree, Kurt never has to guess what I'm thinking. Just like we encourage the kids to do, I use my words to communicate my feelings. But even when Kurt wholeheartedly disagrees with me, he never tells me I'm stupid or wrong. He allows me to have my own feelings, just like I allow him to have his and the kids to have theirs. It's okay to be angry or sad, but it's not okay to retreat from everyone else and go pout in your room.

I know couples who do that. The wife gets mad because she thinks her husband should know what she's feeling. I think lots of people hurt themselves and their marriages when they expect their spouses to know their thoughts when they haven't taken the time to communicate directly.

I did that in my first marriage. I expected my husband to understand what I was feeling without ever telling him. He expected the same thing from me—and when I didn't meet his unspoken needs, he found someone else who apparently did.

That's why the rule in our house is, if you don't talk about your feelings and then the other person doesn't respond the way you want, it's your problem, not the other person's. Kurt always knows what I'm thinking. I'm an open book. I don't play games waiting for him to figure me out. I tell him.

I'm the same way with my girlfriends. They know when I'm mad, because I tell them. I don't do any of that "I'm not talking to her" stuff. The "use your words" rule applies outside the house too.

For example, I recently invited one of my friends to come over and eat with us on a Sunday afternoon. At 1:30, when she should have been arriving, she texted me to say she had just woken up and she planned to just relax the rest of the day. She's single and doesn't have kids, so she can do that.

I texted her back: *So at 1:30 you text that you aren't going to be where you promised to be when I made a meal. Who does that?*

She replied, *Are you mad at me?*

Was I mad at her? Yes, I was. So I texted her back and let her know that, although the meal would get eaten and life would go on, I was not happy that she hadn't cared enough to come over after she had said she would.

I was very clear, so that the next time my friend will know she should either not agree to come if she thinks she might change her plans at the last minute, or she'll know that I expect her to show up. If the same thing happens again, we'll both know that it wasn't because she didn't know my expectations.

I know that might sound harsh, but I think it's worse when expectations aren't made clear. When people aren't sure what you're thinking and they don't know how their actions have affected you, then they're left to guess or play little "I'm not talking to you" games. Life's too short.

I told Jesse the same thing when she started dating. If she clearly explains to her boyfriend what she wants out of a relationship, how she wants to be treated, and what her expectations are, they'll both know when he does and doesn't meet them. And when he doesn't, she won't have to wonder whether she caused the confusion.

I've learned the hard way at the kids' schools that communication and expectations have to be clear. For example, I never want my kids to be put in a position where they're bringing things home for their dad to autograph. Yet there are always those who try to send something home with the kids. We've even gone into parent-teacher conferences and had teachers pull out stuff and ask to have it signed. How professional is that?

That's why every year when I meet the kids' teachers for the first time, I bring it up. "I don't know if you know, but her dad is Kurt Warner. I need for you to help me make her life as normal as possible."

I tell them about the no-autograph rule—that our house is an autograph-free zone. If Jada has a friend whose dad who is a tax accountant, I don't send my taxes to school with Jada and ask her to have her friend take them home to her dad. It's not my kids' job to do that.

I ask the teachers to please address it if they see something inappropriate in that regard going on in the classroom. Not only am I communicating my concerns about my kids, but I am also communicating my expectations of the teachers.

As parents, we may not do everything right, but I think one thing we've always done well is communicate what we're thinking. That's why we have the rules in the first place. They're our shorthand way of communicating our expectations to each other and to our children. The fact that the kids were able to state them so clearly for the *New York Times* article shows they're hearing what we're trying to get across. The fact that others were so intrigued with our rules might have less to do with the actual rules and more to do with their own challenges in clearly articulating their values and expectations for their own families. If that's the case, I hope they borrow our rules—not to impose some kind of legalism in their family but instead to use them as a place to start their own conversations.

My kids will tell you that we don't keep secrets from them. I am open and honest with Jesse about everything, including my relationship with Kurt—that we lived together and that we had premarital sex. And I'm also honest when I tell her, "I want better for you."

I'm not going to hide anything. I understand there are lots of parents who don't want to talk about those kinds of subjects with their sons or daughters, and that's their choice. But my hope is that if I regularly communicate my expectations as well as my experiences—both good and bad—my children will learn from me. I want them to learn from my mistakes so they can be better than I am.

I do this outside of the home as well. People who've heard me give my testimony are shocked that I share so openly. But why not? Those things have already happened, and God already knows about them, so it doesn't bother me. My hope is that, like my kids, others can learn from my experience.

CHAPTER 16

a brief note on notes

{ KURT }

At the beginning of the 2008 season, there were no guarantees that I would be the Cardinals' starting quarterback. In 2007, second-year starter Matt Leinart had broken his collarbone, so I had taken over for the last eleven games of the season. But Matt had healed, and many thought he deserved his spot back. In fact, there was a lot of pressure on coach Ken Whisenhunt to start Leinart—because he was the future of the franchise. But I still felt I was good enough to deserve the starting position.

Before the season, Whisenhunt told me I would have a fair opportunity to compete for the job. But just as Brenda has some trust issues based on her past experiences, I have some trust issues based on mine. In the past, coaches have promised me a fair shot, but then for various reasons they didn't deliver on that promise. So, I was hopeful, but I knew nothing was guaranteed.

Of course, we all know the end of the story. Whisenhunt

kept his word, I earned the spot, and the Cardinals went to the Super Bowl.

After the big game, I sent Coach Whisenhunt the following text message:

> *I'm indebted and appreciative of what you did for me this year. I would have missed out on this, and that would have been terrible.*

I also thought it was important that we still take time to celebrate the season, even though we had lost the Super Bowl. So I wrote:

> *Just wanted to give my two cents' worth on making sure as a team we celebrate this season. We made the mistake of not doing it in St. Louis when we lost, and it made the season seem like a failure.*

Then I closed by saying:

> *For what it's worth, great job, Coach.*

It wasn't long before I got the following text back:

> *Your two cents makes a lot of sense, and I'll make sure we do celebrate what we've done. I appreciate your input because the way it feels right now it would be easy to do just what you said. It's hard to put into words what I feel about you, what you have done for*

*me and this team. I have great respect for how you
handled everything, and I thank God we are on this
journey together.*

People who know me well know I can get pretty emotional
at times. Even now, weeks later, I get choked up reading that
text. The coach's message meant a lot to me.

Notes from the Family

During the season, I can get pretty banged up. Brenda knows
how old my injuries are by the color of the bruise; they
change from bright blue to yellow as the weeks go by. There
are also places on my body where the pads rub, and the more
the season progresses, the more irritated those areas get.

I don't mind the pain—that's part of my job. I think
I'm pretty tough, and I can take it. But it bothers me when
an injury prevents me from doing stuff with my kids. This
year, I played with broken bones in both of my hands and a
hip injury. That meant, while at home, I couldn't do certain
things with my kids such as wrestle or run and play football.
Most times, I could still throw the ball with them. But there
were things I couldn't do, or chose not to do, to make sure
I stayed injury free for the upcoming game.

The kids can see when I'm favoring my bad hand or winc-
ing in pain. They even ask me about the injuries before I leave
for games. "Dad, are you gonna go get beat up?" Or, when
I get home, "Do you have any bruises this week?"

Brenda says it's hard for her to see my injuries, but at least
she understands it's part of the job. We both wonder what

goes through the minds of our youngest children when they see me banged up. How do they make sense of it all?

Sometimes we get a glimpse into what they think. When they say their prayers at night, they'll pray that I don't get hurt. Or sometimes the Babygirls will see a bruise on my arm or leg and say, "Oh, Daddy, owie!" Then they show me theirs—"I got an owie too!"—and we'll all put Dora the Explorer Band-Aids on our owies.

One day, Elijah wanted to write a note to me. Because he can't write yet, he had Brenda do it for him, and then he signed his name. He gave me the note, which said, "Daddy, you are the best player in the NFL. Are you going to keep getting hurt? I love you. Elijah."

Notes like that help me keep my perspective. Though my five-year-old thinks I'm the best player in the league, it's not my stats he's concerned with. It's my physical well-being that is important to him. He doesn't want his daddy hurt.

It didn't surprise me that Elijah sent a note. Sending notes to each other is something Brenda and I have been doing, well, I guess since the first time I told her I loved her on the Magna Doodle. And we still do it. If I leave the house before she wakes up, sometimes I'll leave her a note on the kitchen table. Before each away game, she tucks notes into my playbook, and when I'm traveling, she sends me text messages. I'll also leave notes for our kids—like for Jesse when she's out late and comes in after I go to bed. So notes aren't unusual in our home. They're another way we stay in touch and encourage one another.

This year, there was one note that really stood out for me. It was just a simple one, but it meant everything. I was in

Tampa and unpacking my bags when a paper slipped out. I just assumed it was from Brenda, but I opened it up and got something very different from what I was expecting:

> *Dad, I just wanted to let you know how proud I am of you. I'm so thankful and honored to be your daughter. I'll be praying for you; you deserve everything you want, and probably more. I love you so much. Go Cards! — Jesse*

That was a pretty cool moment. As a parent, you dream so much of the accomplishments your kids will have, and when they happen, you tell them how proud you are. You can get choked up from the emotion. But when one of your kids turns the tables and says she's proud of *you*, well, let's just say I'm glad you can't see me right now, because I get all emotional just thinking about it.

Anyway, I took the note and stuck it under the plastic covering of my playbook. Every time I picked it up, it reminded me to keep a proper perspective and to see beyond the football game.

I didn't plan to mention anything about the note to anyone. But later that day, I had my book with me as I was watching game film. Afterward, I had a press conference, and I took the book with me to the podium. So it was sitting there, and one of the thirty or so reporters saw it and said, "Tell us about the note."

Of course, I got all choked up and explained that it was from my daughter. Someone wanted me to read it, and I did. Several of the reporters wrote about it, and it got a lot of press coverage. It wasn't my intention for it to happen that way, but I know the story touched a lot of people almost as much as the note touched me.

But there was another side to this story, and I thought you might want to hear it directly from Jesse in her own words:

> *I knew Dad was leaving really early the next morning. I didn't have plans to leave him a note or anything. I had just brought down my laundry, and I*

wanted to get something to eat. But I saw his bag lying there.

It reminded me of all the times he'd left me notes on the table. Like when I get home late at night, I'll find a note, and I like it when he does that. So that gave me an idea. We have this really dorky Arizona Cardinals stationery, and I love writing on it because it's so dorky. I don't even know why we have it—it was probably just a random gift from someone.

So I actually wrote a normal note. It was like, "Hey, you're already asleep, so I'll just tell you good night now, and call me when you get there." But as I was writing it, I just started thinking about what a big weekend it was for him, and how far he'd come from a few months earlier when he was competing for his job. I hadn't really paid much attention, in terms of how important it was to him. But he had tried so hard, and he'd broken bones in both his hands and all that—and I just wanted to let him know I was proud of him.

Although I had been getting a lot of unwanted attention at school because of the Super Bowl, it was cool to hear what people were saying about Dad. There were a lot of articles coming out about what a great father he was and all those things. Someone at school would say, "I read a great story about your dad and all this stuff he does for people." So it had been building up, and I felt like I should tell him I was proud. So I thought I would write him a note and tell him that; I threw the first one away and started over.

Two days later at school, we were all joking around in AP Psychology. We didn't want to work on our research papers, so we were goofing off and googling each other's names. I googled my name, and up popped this article that said, "Daughter's Letter Chokes Up Kurt Warner."

My friends were like, "What's that all about?"

"I don't know," I said. "I've never seen this before." So I read it and I said, "I wrote that! I wrote that like two nights ago. I can't believe this is online!"

Then everybody gathered around the computer to see it. "No way!" they said. "That's so cool!"

I was shocked, because you don't expect that something like that would end up on the Internet. I thought it was so strange, because he had been texting me and stuff, but he hadn't mentioned that he'd gotten the letter.

From the articles, I could tell he had just gotten caught with it, and he had gotten all teary-eyed, so it was funny. I texted him and said, "I just read an article that you're reading my note. I didn't even know you got it."

But I thought that was all very cool.

That evening, as I was eating dinner in my room and wishing I was having dinner with the family, I texted Jesse:

Favorite part of my day: Getting a note from my daughter! Love You.

{ BRENDA }

Writing little notes and cards and hiding them in places where only the intended person can find them is something I started doing back when Kurt and I were dating. Since then, I've written notes or cards to all my kids to encourage them or tell them how much I love them. And now they're starting to do it on their own.

It's not necessarily the length or the words that matter. Some of the best notes I've received were the simplest ones. Like drawings that the little ones did at school and then held out to me in their sticky hands, saying, "I made this for you." Sometimes the most inspiring notes come from those who are least able to write them.

When Zack was born, he was healthy, happy, and normal. At four months old, he had enough thick black hair that I could spike it up on the top of his head. His dimples showed every time he smiled—and he smiled all the time. I loved to kiss, kiss, kiss his chubby cheeks. He had beautiful brown eyes that lit up when I sang to him, and his fat little hands would clap along to the beat. I loved to hold him tight when I rocked him to sleep, and I prayed that he would become all that God had planned for him to be.

Nineteen years later, many people might wonder how that could be possible. How could Zack live out God's plan? Well, I believe that God's plan changed when Zack was dropped, and that God has a new plan for him.

I know when many people see Zack, they see the physical imperfections: the fact that his right foot turns in almost ninety degrees, which is what causes him to stumble and run awkwardly. They see how his right leg is half the size of his left leg because his muscles atrophied from the brain damage.

But that's not what I see.

What I see are those same dimples, though now they're hidden by his manly stubble. I see a young man who inspires everyone who knows him because he never gives up and just keeps trying, no matter what. How can any of the kids complain about something trivial when Zack never complains in the face of so much hardship? I also see his joy when he listens to his music and when someone stops long enough for him to share it with them.

What I see is that Zack is perfect the way he is. Yes, I would give my life to give him his sight back. I'd exchange my breath for his complete healing. But even without those things, Zack isn't anything less. In fact, he is so much more. He doesn't know it, but *he* is the reason that Kurt and I do so many of the things we do. Like our hospital visits. Whether it's holding sick babies, delivering baskets to children, or visiting with the parents of a teen who has just been diagnosed with a fatal disease, the reason we do it is because of Zack. Our Disney trips? Those are because of Zack too. The Little Angel casket program in St. Louis? Zack was the inspiration for that, too.

So when I see Zack, I see so much more than other people see. And because I know that Zack is behind so many of the programs we've done through our foundation, I can also see how God still has a plan for his life, even if it isn't the one Zack was born with.

Recently, I was invited to speak, and I wanted to share

Zack's story. As I was preparing, I kept thinking about all the things I wanted to share about Zack. I had a long list, but then another question occurred to me: If he could, what would Zack want to share about himself?

Over the next few days, as I made dinner, ran errands, or just had a few minutes to myself, this question would haunt me. What would Zack say if he could write a letter to the world? What would he want us to know about him?

Finally, one day, I sat down at the computer and wrote a letter from Zack. The words are mine, but I believe Zack's heart is in them.

Here's Zack's note:

Dear World,

I don't know you, but I want to.

I love meeting new people who soon feel like friends to me. I don't like everyone, though. I don't like people who are so busy and hurried. They squeeze by me in doorways or rush by my shoulder to get somewhere. I don't see you coming 'cause my eyes don't work.

Please just slow down. Slow down and you can smell the coffee at the Starbucks on every corner. Slow down and you can hear the baby laughing in the stroller. It will make you smile, I'm sure. Slow down and you can see me.

I can't see you, but I don't care. See, friend, when I was born, I could see. Something bad happened to me. Now I don't see so well. My mom cried a lot.

I think she thinks my life would be better if I could see. But really, I am happy being me. I wake up with no worries. Not like my sister, who worries about pimples, boyfriends, and college exams. Or my dad, who has to go to work every day so he can bring home money for me to buy another radio. Or even my mom, who worries about looking older and being fat. I love them all for who they are inside all of that. The best thing about being me is that I don't see if you are fat, old, ugly, rich, or poor. I just like you.

I want you to know that sometimes things happen that shake our world. We need each other. I need someone to make my meals for me and lay out my clothes for the day. Some people need someone to give them a dollar to make ends meet. There are some who need a hug because something bad happened. Slow down to see (or feel) what someone needs. One day you are the person who gives. One day you might be the person who needs.

Remember me when you want to give up. Remember I didn't.

Remember me when you think life is hard. Remember my life is.

Remember me when you want to hurry through life. Remember me, and slow down!

Love me,
Zack

Writing the note helped me to think from Zack's perspective, but I didn't want to leave it at that. So, before the event, I took the note and had it printed on card stock so I could give one to each person in the audience. I hoped it would be a reminder to them of the things that I said about Zack.

Though I gave the speech months ago and people were touched by Zack's story, I didn't expect to hear anything more about it. But recently I met someone who had attended that speech, and she said she has Zack's note hanging on her refrigerator as a daily reminder of his story. Another person told me that he saved the note in a special place and occasionally takes it out to read as a way of remembering what an inspiring person Zack is.

But there is another person who tucks that note in a special place and occasionally takes it out and reads it too. Before Kurt left to play an away game against the Philadelphia Eagles last season, I took one of the copies of Zack's note that I had prepared for my speech and I put it in an envelope. I labeled the envelope "Perspective" and slipped it into Kurt's bag. It was just my way of helping him remember what was most important. Little did I know how important it would be to him.

Kurt said that he found the note before the game, but it took on new meaning afterward. That Thanksgiving night, the Cardinals lost to the Eagles 48–20. Kurt threw three interceptions, and like all of his losses he took it hard. But after the game, he found the note that he had tucked back into the "Perspective" envelope, and he later told me it really helped him to have the proper perspective on the game. The note is still in Kurt's bag today as a reminder of what's really the most important thing.

Of all my kids, Zack may be the least capable of writing a note, but it looks like when he does, he is the one who is most capable of inspiring, motivating, and encouraging others. If that's true, I can't imagine a more important note.

CHAPTER 17

Aerosmith family vacation

{ KURT }

After a losing football game, I usually head straight to the locker room. I need a few minutes to clear my head and process what just happened. So, although I sometimes wave at Brenda and the kids after a win, I never do it after a loss.

But after the Super Bowl, even though we had lost, I ran over to say hi to my kids. As Brenda mentioned in a previous chapter, she wasn't expecting me to do that. Nevertheless, I did it because I knew the kids would be upset and I knew what they were thinking: *Dad lost. Oh, my gosh—Dad lost the Super Bowl!*

Although I was extremely disappointed, I ran over smiling. I not only wanted to teach them a lesson, but I also wanted to convince myself. "It's okay; it's going to be okay. It's just a game; I love you all, and I'll talk to you in a little while." I wanted them to know that everything would be fine and that I loved them.

Like many of our rules, there was nothing profound in

what I did. It was a simple thing. I wanted my kids to know I cared about how they felt. But in retrospect, I hope that heading straight to them instead of to the locker room reinforced one of my personal rules. For me, family comes first.

In many respects, my life has become what my kids enjoy. We're out here in Arizona and other NFL players say, "You should golf. You have free time; why not golf?" But my kids don't enjoy it, and I don't want to be away from them for five hours, so I don't golf. It's just not a part of my schedule, other than for an occasional charity function. We used to get invited to baseball games all the time, but none of my kids were into it. And if they don't want to do it, I don't want to do it.

I say no to lots of opportunities, not because I don't want to do those things but because they're just not more important than spending time with my family. We've talked about doing the USO tours and a lot of other worthy things, but I always just say no, because I don't want to be away from my kids for that long.

So yes, sometimes loving your family means giving up the things you want to do at the moment in favor of the greater family good. Brenda and I struggle with this as we try to balance our roles, so it's no wonder our kids do too.

We're constantly trying to teach them that sometimes you have to give up some of what you want so your sibling can have some too. Sometimes it's as simple as sharing the last Tootsie Pop; other times, it means keeping your hands to yourself when you want to grab your brother's toy. But it almost always means putting your needs on hold so you can honor the needs of your brother or sister.

We reinforce that by making the kids spend time together. For example, Jesse has always been very protective of Zack, and she still is. When they were younger, she was often his eyes—walking him around the playground or helping him up the stairs. She didn't always want to do it, but there was a special trust there. Maybe because they were both kids, Zack could trust her differently than he could adults. Zack was always on Jesse's right arm.

Right now, Zack is at the mental age where girls have cooties, so he doesn't want to go places with Jesse or talk to her as much as he did in the past. And she misses that. But sometimes, he still tells her things he won't tell Brenda or me. And even now, when he occasionally lets her guide him, his hand still fits on her arm like it used to.

Of course, Jesse will admit that she sometimes took advantage of Zack's blindness by taking things from him without his noticing. But there's no doubt the two of them have a special connection. Last Sunday, they hung out at the church playground because I promised the little ones we'd stop there before going home. Jesse climbed on the tire swing, and Zack pushed her. It was great to see them laughing and playing together, even though they're both young adults. It's that kind of connection we want all of our kids to have with each other and with us.

But kids are not naturally inclined to do that. I don't know about yours, but mine don't always get along. When bickering breaks out among siblings, many parents find it's easiest to just separate the kids. "Go to your room!" they'll tell the offender. Brenda and I do it a little differently; we force them to spend time together.

For example, the other day in the van, Kade was trying to grab something from Jada, and she wasn't happy. "Keep your hands in your lap where they belong," I said, "or you're going to hold hands for ten minutes."

That stopped it; neither child wanted to hold hands with the other one.

The two rules from the *New York Times* article that provoked the most reader response were the one about holding hands for ten minutes and the one that followed: "If you can't get along holding hands, sit cheek to cheek. (If you can't get along cheek to cheek, then it's lips to lips!)"

I think those two got more attention because parents immediately recognized how much the kids would hate having it enforced. But many parents wouldn't want to enforce such a rule because it's simply easier to separate the kids by sending them to different areas of the house. But that doesn't help prepare kids for real life. They will have bosses and coworkers they don't like, but they'll still have to learn how to get along with those people.

We want to teach our kids how to get along with each other and not just how to ignore their siblings when they're being difficult. Forcing them to spend time together does that.

That rule applies to Jesse and Brenda, also. If Jesse gets in trouble, it's not because she missed a curfew or something you would expect from a teenager. If Jesse gets in trouble, it's because she got into an argument and lost her temper—usually with her mom. When that happens, her punishment is to spend more time with her mother. I admire Brenda for doing that. It would probably be easier on Brenda if she just sent

Jesse to her room. But by forcing Jesse to spend time with her, it teaches Jesse that she can't run away from her problems. Jesse can't go and sulk; she has to work it out.

Because of Zack's special needs, Jesse is really our first child to go through the teen years, and she's taught us a lot. One of the things we learned was that the older she got, the more she wanted to spend time with her friends. Some of our rules cramped her style. For example, our insistence that she be home for dinner every night often meant she couldn't stay at a friend's house as long as she wanted. We understood, but eating dinner together is an important rule in our home, and we weren't going to let up on it. So that caused a few arguments. "Nobody sits with their family every night at dinner!" she'd tell us.

We solved the problem by telling Jesse she could still spend time with her friends but she had to bring them to our house for dinner. She ended up bringing lots of friends over.

All of her close friends, except one, come from divorced homes. Jesse saw the things they had to go through with two houses, having to go back and forth between them, and it made her appreciate how hard their lives were sometimes. But when her friends got to our house and saw two parents who loved each other, a family that prayed together, and a conversation that included everyone at the table, they seemed to really appreciate the family dinners, which they didn't have in their own homes. They would eat at our house once and then want to come back because they liked the experience. Their appreciation rubbed off on Jesse, and slowly she began to appreciate it too. Now, as she looks ahead to college next year, she realizes that her dinners at home are numbered, and she's changed the way she feels about that rule.

Here's what she said recently:

> *I look at my friends who are only children, and I guess there are probably some perks to being the only one, because you get all the attention. But now that I'm going to college, I realize it's a real blessing to have a houseful of people who are always there. And it's been awesome to look up to my parents through all of this. I understand why they make us do some of the things we have to do. I can't even believe I'm saying that, because six months ago I wouldn't have. But now that I'm realizing more and more, it's really cool.*

As a parent, hearing your daughter say something like that lets you know things are working. Some of what you're trying to teach is sinking in. And it makes enforcing the rules—even when they're hard to enforce—worth doing.

{ BRENDA }

Kurt talked about how we sometimes use our rules as a way to force our kids to get along, but that's not our first choice. We'd rather teach them about getting along by simply spending time together as a family and doing the things we all enjoy.

We have a house in Cabo San Lucas, Mexico, which is such a luxury. It's absolutely the most beautiful place I've ever stayed. But when we go there, we make it a point not to have a phone, not to have Internet access, and not to have video games. There's no Xbox or arcade games like we have in Phoenix. Cabo is strictly about family time.

When we watch movies, the rule is we do it together. That means they have to be PG and something we can all agree on. One of our favorite things to do is play board games. We always choose games like Uno and Guesstures, games that every child can participate in.

We also have more opportunities to just hang out in public as a family when we're in Cabo. We take walks together and sometimes even go downtown. Though Kurt is still recognized, people don't seem to care like they do in the States.

In some ways, we've even expanded our family. While in Cabo, a local woman stays at the house and helps us. Her name is Dulce, and the kids just love her. Sometimes Dulce will bring her children over, and though they don't speak English, they love to play with our kids. The kids spend all day playing, laughing, and swimming. When they need to communicate, they use sign language. Last week, Dulce called our house in Phoenix, and when one of the Babygirls heard me talking to her, she asked about Dulce's daughter. "How's Jasmine doing?"

We believe that spending time together and making memories like this as a family will bring the kids together even after we're gone.

Aerosmith Vacation

The inspiration for our family vacations in Cabo began with a trip we took several years ago. We were living in St. Louis, and

it was after the Super Bowl win, so it was the first big vacation we could afford. Rather than heading to a destination
where we would each end up going our separate ways, or hir-
ing a sitter to watch the younger kids while we took the older
ones, we decided to do something we could all experience as
a family.

A friend recommended a tour bus company, so I called
them to arrange a bus and driver for a week. The plan was—
well, there was no plan. We would give the driver a general
idea of what we wanted to do, and where we wanted to go
each day, but we held the option to change our minds at any
moment.

The bus was too big to pick us up at the house, so the
driver had to meet us in the parking lot of our church. We
were scheduled to meet him early in the evening, and it had
just gotten dark when we got there with all our bags. I hadn't
told the kids we were taking a bus, but even if I had, they
never would have expected what showed up.

As the bus pulled into the lot, the first thing we noticed
was how big it was. Much bigger than even Kurt or I had
expected. The driver had turned on the outside lights of the
bus, so it was all lit up. The kids couldn't believe what they
were seeing. We soon learned that the bus was Aerosmith's old
tour bus. And it was seriously decked out. Big-screen TVs,
bunks for the kids, and a beautiful bathroom. There was also
a kitchen area and a bedroom in the back. As a kid, all you
know are those yellow school buses; you can't imagine a bus
like this.

We left St. Louis, and our first stop would be the next day

in North Carolina. As the bus merged onto the highway, the kids were picking out their bunks, and they discovered that each bunk had a separate TV that dropped down. So they had fun trying out all the remotes and getting used to where they'd be spending the next few nights.

Kurt and I headed to the back room. There was a queen-size bed that basically filled the room, and there were mirrors everywhere.

For the next seven days, we drove wherever we wanted. We spent a night in North Carolina and a day in Charlotte. In Charleston, South Carolina, we rode the trolley. None of us had ever been on a trolley before. So we hopped on and then got off at the museum. We also visited the aquarium and ate lunch at a local restaurant.

Every day, we just did what we wanted. If we saw something that looked interesting, we'd ask the driver to stop, and we'd hop off and go exploring. After Charleston, we headed to Parris Island, South Carolina, where I had gone to boot camp. Because Kurt was a celebrity, we got a VIP tour, and the kids got to see all the things I used to do. Like fire M16s. Or do water safety, where I had to learn to take off my camouflage uniform and float with it.

We also got to eat in the mess hall. At the time I trained there, we had only twenty minutes to finish our meals. The clock started when the first recruit walked in. Because I was always at the maximum allowable weight for my height, I was considered a "fat private" and thus was always the last one through the line. In a line of sixty-two recruits, that meant I had less time to eat than anyone else. The servers also knew that the fat privates never got dessert. Now there I was, getting a VIP tour of the place where I had never been allowed to finish my meal.

It was a great opportunity to tell some of my stories to my kids. I wouldn't go so far as to say it's a rule at our house, but it's something Kurt and I do a lot of—tell stories about our growing up years. It's a way to connect the kids to our past and help remind them of some of the Midwestern values we grew up with.

After I had told so many Marine stories on that trip, Jesse said, "Mom, you are so cool!" It think that was the first and last time she ever thought I was cool.

Following Parris Island, we went to Pensacola Beach, where I had met my first husband. As a family, we played on the same beach where I had worked as a Marine.

Our stops took us from Florida to Tennessee and then back to St. Louis. We tried to do something special in every town we stopped in. In Memphis, we ate at a restaurant that was famous for its grits. Another one of our favorite stops was Bubba Gump Shrimp Company, where we played a *Forrest Gump* trivia game. Since that trip, we eat at Bubba Gump's every chance we get (most recently while we were in New Orleans) because it brings back so many good memories.

Being on the road made us want to spend time together. If we had been on another kind of vacation, one kid would have wanted to go to the pool while another would have wanted a different activity. We couldn't do that in the bus; it was forced family time—card games, board games, you name it. It was one of our best vacations ever, and we try to re-create that experience every time we go to Cabo.

Our house in Phoenix is often loud, crazy, and chaotic, with people going their own way. But there are moments when I get a glimpse of what true togetherness looks like. My favorite moments are when togetherness happens naturally.

Like sometimes I'll walk into Zack's room, and he'll be watching cartoons on the big-screen TV in his room, and Jada, Elijah, and the Babygirls will join him. Zack gets really close to the screen when he watches, so his favorite thing to do is squat in front of the TV. The other kids will all sit in a row next to him. A new show will come on, and one of them will say, "Zachary, I don't like this one. Will ya turn it?"

Without a word, Zack will stand up and turn the channel for them. He just serves them. Zack wants to be needed, and in those moments, he feels useful.

I love that.

It's a reminder of why we do the rules, the forced time together, and the family vacations. Those are all about the kids learning to love and value each other. Thirty years from now, when they have spouses and kids of their own, I hope they'll still find time to sit in the same room next to each other and enjoy being together.

CHAPTER 18

your family
will always be there

{ KURT }

Even when you're famous, there are constant reminders that
your fame isn't all you think it is and that it won't last forever.
For example, I was in St. Louis around the time that baseball
player Mark McGwire broke the single-season home run
record. Obviously, his name and image were all over the news.
Occasionally, I'd be walking down the street, and someone
would stop me and say, "Hey, Mark! Congrats on your home
run last night." It always made me laugh, because the person
recognized me but just made the wrong connection.

It made more sense when the confusion was with Trent
Green, who at the time was the Rams' starting quarterback.
People would recognize me, and they'd say, "Hey, Trent, I'm
your biggest fan!"

Before the Cardinals started playing so well in 2008,
I even had a few people who confused me with backup
quarterback Matt Leinart. I never wanted to make them feel
bad in those situations, so when they said, "Hey, Matt," I just

waved and said hello. When they asked me to sign some-thing, I did. But I'm sure some of them were confused as they walked away, wondering why Matt Leinart had signed Kurt Warner's name.

I can understand how that confusion happens with fans. Because they've seen you on TV, they know they recognize you when they see you in person, but it's out of context. What I don't always understand is when a *coach* doesn't know basic things about me, such as how to spell my name.

I once worked with a coach for two seasons, and halfway through the second year, he said, "All right, let's go, C.W."

Like my name is spelled with a *C*.

After practice ended, I called him on it, and he made some excuse, but the truth was that he just didn't know how to spell my name. And that wasn't the first time a coach had made that mistake. One year, around Christmas, a coach left me a note asking me to sign something for him. The note was addressed to Curt.

It's not only the coaches I work with who have trouble with my name. In 1999, the agency that represented me called and asked if I was available for an interview. Someone in the media wanted to interview me about the 1983 Sugar Bowl. I thought it was an odd request, but in this business, you see a lot of odd things. It was my agency asking, so I fig-ured they thought it was a good opportunity for me. "Sure, I'll do it," I told the woman who was setting it up, "but I was only twelve years old at the time."

Turns out, they didn't want me after all. They really wanted Curt Warner, who was a running back for the Penn

State team that won the 1983 Sugar Bowl and who went on to play for the Seahawks and the Rams in the NFL.

Those are funny little things that keep me humble, but they're also reminders that celebrity comes and goes. Fans can be fickle, depending on how things go on the field. Coaches come and go, depending on the whims of owners. And players come and go, on the decision of coaches and general managers. Although I value the relationships I make in the industry, I realize that one day my career will end and many of those relationships will too.

That's what makes it so easy to put my family first and to sacrifice for them. My relationship with my family won't last a year or two and be gone; it'll last for generations. From that aspect alone, it makes prioritizing time with my family a worthwhile investment.

That's something Brenda and I try to teach our kids. It's easy for them to think their friendships are their most important relationships, which is one reason Brenda talks about their relationships with their friends when the kids accompany her on away-game trips. She'll ask them, "Which friends do you have now that you think you will still have in ten years?" It's a great question, and one that helps our kids to prioritize their relationships.

Jada, for example, will come home from school and be upset about something another kid said while making fun of her on the bus. She'll be in a terrible mood and take it out on the whole family. At those times, we sit down and try to talk about it. Often she'll confess that she doesn't even know the offender very well. "If he doesn't know you, how could he know the truth about you?" I'll ask. Then I'll remind her, "It's not important what people on the bus say; it's important what people closest to you say."

I think of those conversations with my kids every time I read a negative story in the newspaper or hear one on TV. Those people don't know me personally. They don't know whether it was a play I called or one called by someone else. They didn't see what I saw when I threw the ball. So whatever they're saying isn't as important to me as what those closest to me are saying. I can't let the media dictate the kind of day or season I'm going to have.

Knowing which relationships are the most important helps us know where we should spend our energy. For me, it's with my wife and kids. That's why I invest a lot of time trying to understand who they are, discovering their interests, and supporting them in their passions.

I've already mentioned that Zack likes to pick up trash. But other things get him excited too. Recently, he was stuck on finding where his teacher lived. For weeks we drove around looking for her house, but he didn't have any idea where it was. It would have been easy to shut him down and tell him how stupid it was to be driving around aimlessly. Instead, I got in the car with him and said, "Which way do you think we should go?"

"It's up there, by that street," he said, and I went in the direction he pointed.

Zack didn't have an address, an area of town, or any other location information. He only knew there was a black truck parked in the driveway. Again, it would have been so easy to say, "Well, Zack, it's that one right there. They just put the truck in the garage." But I took his interests seriously. I never belittled him, because I could see how much he cared about finding it. I don't know why it was so important to him to search for her house, and it wasn't particularly important to me, but I cared because Zack cared.

That's what I want the kids to know: Sacrifice begins when it's not what you want but what the other person wants.

Brenda made a similar sacrifice for Zack the other night. He had been to the hardware store that day with our friend Rory and saw that a shopping cart from the nearby CVS Pharmacy had been left in the wrong parking lot. We're not even sure how Zack saw it, but it bothered him. So all day he kept talking about it. He wanted to go back to the parking lot and return it to the rightful store.

Brenda could easily have said, "Zack, just go to bed. Someone probably already returned the cart," but she took his concerns seriously. And even though she was already in her pajamas and ready for bed, she drove Zack to the hardware store and looked around until she spotted the misplaced cart—it was still there.

Because she didn't want to get out of the car in her pajamas, she told Zack to get the cart and follow her as she slowly drove the van across the drive that connected the two parking lots and then up to the CVS door. It must have been quite a sight to see this visually impaired boy pushing the cart behind the van—although Brenda had to be praying that no one saw it. Once Zack had returned the cart to its proper spot, he went home and slept peacefully.

Occasionally, I see parents who dismiss their kids' concerns or belittle their children's interests. I never want to be that guy. I want to be the guy who supports the passions of those I love. For Zack, that may be his teacher's address, shopping carts, or picking up trash. For Jesse, it's art, music, and acting. My role as a father is to help my kids discover what makes them come alive and then help them pursue their God-given talents.

We want our kids to do the same with each other. That's another one of our rules. The kids have to support their siblings' interests and activities even if they're not interested themselves. So we require them to attend their brothers' and sisters' events. We think that does two things: First, it supports each child's unique differences and accomplishments; and second, those very activities broaden each child's perspective. Although Kade may not be interested in cheerleading, for example, when he attends Jada's competitions, he not only supports his sister in what she loves, but he's also exposed to something he wouldn't otherwise choose to do.

The same goes for my support of Brenda. As a former Marine and a career woman, Brenda had a very full life before she had kids. Though being a mom to seven kids offers its own rewards, sometimes she is so busy taking care of others that she forgets to take care of herself. I know it's easy in those moments for her to say, "God just wants me to be a mom." But I don't think she has to. I remind her how blessed we are to be in a position where we can support her other passions—such as photography. I think she needs to pursue her own interests, to do something that gives her a feeling of worth.

It's too easy to get stuck in a rut where you're just somebody's mom and somebody's wife rather than fully become the person God created you to be.

I think God made Brenda to be creative. To feel completely alive, she needs to use her creativity to feed her passions. That's why I push her. It's one of the things she tries to suppress, but it's what drives her. And I want Brenda to model that drive for our daughters.

Jesse, like Brenda, is also very creative. She's taught herself both piano and guitar. She sings beautifully, and she also acts. I'm not artsy in that regard. I don't draw, I don't play music, I can't sing, and I can't act. But through watching Jesse, and through some of the traveling we've done, I've come to appreciate artistic talent. I love Broadway. I love musicians and watching them do their thing. My appreciation for the arts has come from trying to support Jesse and Brenda in their passions.

When we invest ourselves in the interests of our family members, we not only support them and make those relationships a priority, but we also improve ourselves and become a little more well-rounded in the process.

{ BRENDA }

If there's one thing all my kids agree on, it's that going to Kurt's football games is the worst part of the away-game weekend. Regardless of which child is on the trip, Sunday morning starts with my saying the same thing: "Come on, you need to get up! You need to get ready."

"No . . . no . . . Dad won't even notice if we're there."

"We have to see his game."

"Can't we watch it on TV?"

"No. We're going *to* the game."

"Can we just go for *part* of the game?"

When we get to the stadium, the kids are allowed to go down on the field to see Kurt. He usually comes over, kisses them, and tells them that he loves them. Sometimes they see other players they know. Neil Rackers, the kicker, is referred to as "Jacob's dad." Dirk Johnson is Haven's dad. Of course, all the kids love Larry Fitzgerald because he always talks and jokes with them.

The other day, someone asked Jesse if it was cool to go onto the field before the game. She told him, "It's like visiting your dad's office. There are all of my dad's middle-aged friends, and he's only friends with all the special-teams dorks. But yeah, it's fun because they're all funny, and we love them."

Of course, when Elijah goes, he just wants to hang with his buddy Larry.

Then we go up to our seats, and absolutely nobody ever wants to watch the game. Jesse's constantly going for food, and she has to go to the bathroom twelve times. She just doesn't want to sit in her seat. Zachary puts his headphones on so he can listen to music and not hear me cheering the entire time. Kade and Elijah each play their Nintendo DS games, and Jada has an American Girl doll that she undresses, dresses, and creates hairstyles for.

So why do we do it? Why do we make the kids go? Because we believe it's important for family members to support each other, even when it's not something they want to do.

In this case, we do it for Kurt. He only gets about an hour and fifteen minutes with us the night before the game, and that's not a lot of time, so he likes knowing we're there the next day for the game. He knows, as well as I do, that the kids don't care about the game, but nevertheless, it makes him happy knowing we're in the stands. And as a family, we support each other by attending each other's events. Even if it means getting out of bed on a Sunday morning to go to a game that no one but me is watching.

It's not just about Kurt and football, either. The kids go to each other's activities all the time. When Kade had his fourth-grade choir concert, the other eight of us came to watch him sing his three songs. When Elijah had his preschool performance, the entire Warner family was in the audience. Jesse's plays aren't always appropriate for the younger ones, but Zack loves to go and listen to them. When Jada gets to go, she loves seeing her sister on stage. Even if there is an event like pasta night or a carnival at one of the kids' schools, the whole family packs into the van and attends. It's just another opportunity for us to spend time together as a family.

Those outings also serve another purpose. They offer real-life occasions for the kids to practice the rules we verbally teach—rules they can use when they have their own families. Raising Kade means that I am bringing up a boy who will one day be a man and the head of a household. So, even now, I tell him he is responsible for taking care of his little brother and sisters. When we're at an event, it gives him an opportunity to practice being responsible by helping younger ones out of the van or by holding their hands when we cross the street.

Kade is a big kid now, and someday he will be a huge man. We know he'll have a lot of power and strength, so we want him to be able to control that strength and his emotions. So I also use those opportunities to reinforce how we treat one another. When we're all headed to the door, I remind Kade to let his sisters walk in first.

Of course, he doesn't always understand. I often hear him ask, "Why?" But then his questions become a teaching moment.

"Because I want you to learn to treat ladies with respect."

Maybe because of my military background, I often look at our family as a troop: We're only as strong as our weakest link. One of the things I try to teach the kids is that whoever is strong needs to help whoever is weak. So when someone's going through a hard time, we're all in it together. If Dad is struggling on the football field, we rally around him. When Kade broke his finger, we helped him cut his meat at the dinner table and use scissors for his homework. When Jesse is rehearsing for a play or preparing for an audition, we're her audience. When the kids swim in our backyard pool, it's a constant reminder that the older ones have to watch the younger ones.

It's not that we're delegating the child-rearing responsibilities to the older kids, because we're not. But it is a reminder that—as family—we're all in this together. If you're the stronger one, you take care of the weaker ones, because someday you will be the weaker one. Even though Kade is big and will grow bigger, he will still have moments of weakness. He will need his little sisters one day. It may be when he's thirty years old, but there will still come a day when he will need them.

I'm sure part of the reason I feel so strongly about our kids' being there for each other comes from losing my parents in the prime of their lives. In an instant, half my family was gone—there were no longer four of us; now there were only two. My sister and I had to learn to take care of each other and be a family without our parents.

Fortunately, my kids have an entire group to take care of them. I want them to know that it's more than just Kurt and me supporting them; there's a whole family who will lift them up and carry them throughout their lives. We're a troop, and we go forward together. We're not leaving anybody behind.

Some people make friendships in childhood and remain lifelong friends, and I think that's beautiful. But it's also rare. For our family, with our crazy lifestyle, and as many times as we've had to move, the odds are against our kids having those types of relationships as adults. On the other hand, the odds are 100 percent that their siblings will be there to the end—from crib to casket—so we make family a priority. And that's a rule.

CHAPTER 19

but the greatest of these is love

{ KURT }

In the early days, when playing in the NFL was a faraway dream, I would pray a simple prayer: *God, just give me a job. I don't care what it is. I don't care how hard I have to work. Just make sure there's always a job so I can provide for my family.* That's all I asked. I just wanted to be a good provider.

Obviously, God has answered that prayer in ways I could never have expected.

I started this book by saying I wanted you to know the real Kurt and Brenda, not the two-dimensional characters often portrayed in the media or on blogs. By now you can see—we're really pretty normal.

Yes, my career did change some things. I do have a few trophies, but they are tarnished and hidden on the back of the shelf, behind Kade's Pop Warner trophies. And, yes, I do have a Super Bowl ring. But the last time I saw it was when our cleaning lady held it up and showed it to me. She'd just found it under the sofa along with a stray Lego piece and Brenda's deodorant.

"Is this important?" she asked.

A few people might read this book and think that because I have a Super Bowl ring or whatever, I have all the answers. Nothing could be further from the truth. I do have *some* answers—some answers that have worked for the Warner family—the rules we've described in this book. But I know there isn't just one way to accomplish a goal. Brenda's parents met each other, and six weeks later they got married. They were happily married until the day they died—probably holding hands. Other couples waited ten years to get married, and their marriages also worked. There isn't just one way to do it right.

When people say "one size fits all," they're lying. Every year, my team has to order me a special helmet because I have a small head. (I can just hear Brenda making jokes right now.) There's no "one size" for marriage, either. People say being married in the NFL is very hard. Well, for Brenda and me, it hasn't been that hard. It hasn't been nearly as hard as when we didn't have money and were raising the kids in the basement of her parents' house. That was the stuff that bonded us together. That's when we established who we were. We learned the principles each of us stood for and what we as a couple stood for. During those early days of struggling, we discovered what kind of parents we were and how we would handle things like money.

Comparatively, those were the hard days. But I wouldn't trade them for anything. They got us where we are today. Because we made it through those early struggles, I don't have any questions about whether Brenda married me for money.

When she married me, I didn't have any. Those struggles also got me to this point in my faith. During those lean years, I learned to trust God no matter how impossible the circumstances seemed. Brenda and I grew together in our faith and in our roles as spouses and parents.

But the fact that "the experts" say it's hard for professional athletes to be married, or because other NFL marriages haven't worked out, doesn't change anything about Brenda and me. We know who we are, and we know where we came from. Wherever we go from here, we're going together.

The rules we have as a couple and as a family give us a foundation, and a confidence, for the future. Writing this book has made me think about them more than I ever had before.

But I don't want you to think we have a set of strict laws or codes and anyone who breaks them is immediately in the doghouse. That's not how it works. In fact, as I look back over this book and see all the rules, it reminds me of another big book of rules—the Bible. I don't want to get all religious on you here—because I'm not at all—but hang with me for a minute.

Some people look at the Bible and think it's a bunch of dos and don'ts and if you mess up, you go to hell. In fact, even in Jesus' day, people were so desperate to make sure they didn't break a law that they wrote them on their doorposts and the men carried them around in little boxes. There were hundreds, maybe thousands, of rules at that time. So one day, a guy comes up and asks Jesus, "Out of all the rules, which one is the most important?"

It was a trick question. The guy was a legal expert, and he

knew the minute Jesus picked one of the rules, it would mean the others weren't as important.

But Jesus, he was a smart guy. And he had a great answer: "'You must love the LORD your God with all your heart, all your soul, and all your mind.' This is the first and greatest commandment" (Matthew 22:37-38).

That's the same answer I would give you if you asked me about the most important rule in my life. I love that Jesus says we should love God so passionately. It's not like some girly "let's hold hands" kind of love; it's full contact. Jesus wants us to love God with our entire being—our heart, soul, and mind. That's how I want to love him.

But Jesus wasn't done. He added another rule: "The second is equally important: 'Love your neighbor as yourself'" (Matthew 22:39).

By *neighbor*, I don't think Jesus meant just the people who live on either side of your house. He meant everyone—family, friends, and the people who come up and ask me for autographs. He didn't say that we had to give them everything we own or stop being who we are and be who they want. He said we need to love them. Love them just as much as we love ourselves. Do for them what we would want done for us.

That's what all the rules in this book—the rules we have for ourselves, our marriage, and our kids—are all about. Brenda and I want to love God passionately with our hearts, souls, and minds, and we want to treat others like we treat ourselves. We also want to teach our kids to do the same. I hope that's what you get out of this book. The rules are the means to help us love God and each other.

I know that's not sophisticated advice. It's just simple. But all I can say is that I want my wife and kids to know I love Jesus.

And I want them to know I also love them—all the time.

In my marriage, I want Brenda to know that when I'm mad at her, I love her. When I disagree with her, I love her. When she's angry and irritated with the kids, I love her. When she's beautiful and we're having fun, I love her. And that's the bottom line; I always want her to know how much I care. As long as she knows that, no matter what the circumstances are, I think we'll always be fine.

I believe the same thing with my kids—no matter how I screw up or they screw up, as long as they always know I love them, we're going to be just fine.

I've shared some of the techniques I use to help them know how much I love them. But as I said, every family is different, just as every person is unique. So I am not going to pretend that I have all the answers or the perfect way to make it work for you.

On and off the field, I am drawn to the guys who are the best at what they do. I want to study them and learn from them. And when it comes to loving other people, the guy who does it best is Jesus.

So in my life—in marriage, in parenting, in my foundation—I want to show the love of Jesus all the time. Not by preaching (although I do that occasionally), but instead by trying to do the practical things that Jesus did: Put others first. Serve people. Sacrifice. Invest time in the ones I'm closest to. Look at a person's heart instead of his or her appearance.

Those are the things I want to be the best at—the things I want my whole family to be the best at. But we're never the best the first time we try, which is why we keep working at it.

{ BRENDA }

Relationships aren't easy, even when you're married to a great guy like Kurt. I can tell you now, even after I had dated Kurt for five years, I still didn't know what I was getting into when I said, "I do."

Not long after we were married, he left for Amsterdam to play football for NFL Europe. Then he came back and almost immediately went to St. Louis. I was nine months pregnant, and he called me on a Tuesday night and told me he'd made the Rams. I had to pack up the house in two days. A moving company picked up our stuff on Thursday. On Friday, Jesse, Zack, and I drove to join Kurt in St. Louis. A week later, I gave birth to Kade. So it all happened very quickly.

In those early days, it wasn't a normal marriage. Kurt, who had been around so much while we dated, was suddenly gone once we were married. That wasn't what I expected. Now don't get me wrong. I married the greatest guy in the world, hands down. But it shocked me that our marriage wasn't going to provide the normal little life my parents had. Kurt wasn't going to work a nine-to-five job and have evenings and weekends off.

But I was in, no matter what.

And what a ride it has been. On the inside, I still feel like a little Iowa farm girl, but on the outside, my life resembles the stories I used to read in *People* magazine. Everything is so much bigger and happens so much faster than I could've ever imagined. Kurt's fame attracts unwanted media attention, starstruck fans, and a host of other distractions that take us away from our family more than we'd like. Kurt says he'd never trade what we have now for what we had before. To him, the opportunity to influence and have an impact on so many people is too important.

But would I trade it?

I think about that sometimes.

What would it be like to live with seven kids in a small house in Iowa while Kurt worked for John Deere? I know I'd appreciate the anonymity and the time alone with my family—those are the things I treasure most. Some people, including Kurt, don't believe me when I say I would consider giving up Kurt's celebrity and money. But remember, I was the girl who loved him when he worked at Hy-Vee, lived in my parents' basement, and attended Zack's IEP meetings. At that time, Kurt had no prospects for playing football, let alone for fame or fortune.

So . . . yes. I would trade what we have now for an anonymous slice of Iowa heaven. That's not to say I don't appreciate and value the experiences Kurt's career has given us, because I do. But if I gave that up now, no matter where we went or regardless of what Kurt did, I'd still have the things that make me happy—my faith, my kids, and my husband, who loves me and is devoted to me.

Of course, I'd still want to keep those vacations if I could. . . .

The things I treasure about our life right now are not the

things money can buy; they're the things money *can't* buy—like the opportunity to share our values and our love for Jesus on a national platform. But like the other blessings, this one has come with a few burdens, too. Because we share our love for Jesus, sometimes people's expectations about us change. Either they think we're holier than thou, or because we're Christians, they think we're not fun to hang out with or we're going to judge them. That couldn't be further from the truth. We really just want to love them like God loves us. Because frankly, I don't know how people survive what I've been through without love and faith.

I am so thankful that when I was young, I was part of an amazing youth group that helped me fall in love with Jesus. At my church, I was surrounded by incredible Christian people who just loved the Lord and made me want to love him too. No one tried to force religion on me; instead, it was something I wanted. When I was in ninth grade, I read my Bible a half hour every day—not because anyone forced me to but because I *wanted* to. To me, the Bible wasn't a book of rules; it was a love letter from God.

Sometimes Christians make God look so silly: *"Come on down the aisle. You're the winner. You're the next contestant to get a free trip to heaven."* That's just wrong. Faith isn't a prize you win; it's a relationship you develop and enjoy. When I started dating Kurt, I didn't do silly things to get him to fall in love with me. It was a love that developed over time. When I speak about my faith, I want others to know that my faith is a very real relationship. And that's what I want my kids to have. Faith that is authentic and real, not some goofy prize.

As a parent, I try to give our kids a foundation of faith on which to build their lives. I want my kids to know that God loves them and so do we. Their lives are not accidents. The kids are here for a purpose.

If I hadn't received that foundation growing up, my struggles would have knocked me out. My faith has been tested. But because I knew God has a plan for my life, I trusted him enough to stick it out and see his plan unfold. Of course, it didn't always seem fair—but Jesus dying for me wasn't fair either.

Now, there are days when I'm sitting at Hacienda Rehabilitation and holding a baby who is so sick he needs a tracheotomy, a feeding tube, and oxygen. When I look into his eyes, I think, *This isn't fair to you, just like it wasn't fair to Zack. But God has a plan for you, little one. I've seen him fulfill his purpose in Zack's life.*

In those moments, I am grateful for even the worst things I've gone through; otherwise, I wouldn't be holding and praying for those little babies. The things I've gone through have left me with a drive to help people who are struggling. Sick babies and their worried parents. Welfare moms on food stamps, scraping together enough quarters to buy gas. Single parents and their children who deserve so much more. The poor and disenfranchised who live quiet lives of desperation. The cold, the hungry, and the homeless.

To some people, those are just categories. And maybe in the past, they were to me, too. But now they are real people. Those are the people I vacation with at Disney every year. They're the kids at the local high school, learning to cope with disabilities. They're the parents without money to pay for a casket, and they're the families who open the front door to their own home for the first time.

Those are people I love passionately. I can't help it. I was once just like them, in similar circumstances. I know part of God's plan was to teach me to love them so that one day I would be able to serve them.

When I make my kids do community service, it's not about looking good or having great stories to tell. It's about putting them in situations where they can no longer categorize people. Putting them in situations where they see real people with names and faces and stories. I hope having real relationships with the less fortunate around us will make my kids want to go into the world and make things different. I don't want my kids to just see the world—to go to Africa on a safari. I want them to *change* the world—to go to Africa and feed starving children.

And that's what I hope for you. I hope you will take your own experiences and use them to help the people God has burdened your heart to love. Relationships are never easy— whether we're talking about our faith relationship with God or our relationships with other people. But God is love. And he has created us to love others and to be loved. Some of the worst things you've experienced might be the very things that help you to love the best.

The rules in this book are some of the tools we use to love each other, and the people around us, a little better each day. It's my hope and prayer that some of them will help you to do the same.

NOTES

CHAPTER 2: RED BOOTS AND PINK BATHROBES

1. Adapted from http://www.freerepublic.com/focus/
   f-chat/2168790/posts.

CHAPTER 4: AN INTRODUCTION TO THE WARNER RULES

1. Karen Crouse, "The Rules of the Family," *New York Times*, September
   25, 2008, http://www.nytimes.com/2008/09/
   26/sports/football/26rules.html?ref=football.
2. Philippians 4:13, NKJV

ABOUT THE AUTHORS

KURT AND BRENDA WARNER met when she was a twenty-five-year-old, divorced mother of two, living on food stamps and working her way through nursing school, and he was a twenty-one-year-old backup quarterback at the University of Northern Iowa.

Brenda was certain that Kurt would be scared off by the news that she was a "package deal." Instead, he fell in love with her *and* her kids. On October 11, 1997, they got married. Shortly thereafter, Kurt adopted Brenda's kids, and over the past twelve years, they've added five more children to their family.

In 2001, the Warners established First Things First, a family foundation dedicated to promoting Christian values and positively affecting the lives of those less fortunate. Projects include Baskets of Hope, which delivers baskets of stuffed animals, toys, Bibles, and music to children with life-threatening diseases; Homes for the Holidays, which surprises single-parent, first-time homeowners with complete furnishings for their new homes; and We're Going to Disney World, an annual trip to Walt Disney World for terminally ill children and their families.

Each of the First Things First projects grows out of Kurt and Brenda's own personal experiences and is centered on their life theme of putting faith and family first. To date, the Warners have initiated more than a dozen ongoing projects that affect the lives of people in communities in Arizona, Missouri, and Iowa.

Kurt and Brenda live near Phoenix, Arizona, with their seven children: Zack, Jesse, Kade, Jada, Elijah, Sienna, and Sierra.

JENNIFER SCHUCHMANN is an accomplished writer, trainer, and speaker noted for creative and practical approaches to business and spiritual topics. The author of *Six Prayers God Always Answers*, *Nine Ways God Always Speaks*, and *Your Unforgettable Life*, Jennifer has also written for *Today's Christian*, *The Christian Communicator*, and *Atlanta* magazine. Jennifer lives in Atlanta with her husband, David, and their son, Jordan.

FIRST THINGS FIRST
FOUNDATION

In 2001, Kurt and Brenda Warner established First Things First as a 501(c)(3) public charity. The foundation's mission is to have an impact on people's lives by promoting Christian values, sharing experiences, and providing opportunities to encourage people that all things are possible when we seek to put "first things first." First Things First has actively initiated twelve ongoing projects that bless people in communities in Arizona, Missouri, Iowa, and beyond. Programs include trips to Walt Disney World for ill children, building recreation centers in children's hospitals, teaching the football basics to Special Olympics athletes, and rewarding single parents as they achieve their dreams of home ownership. Each program promotes the Warners' life theme of putting faith and family first.

These programs would not be possible without the support of our community and corporate teammates throughout the years, especially Aaron Rents, American Airlines, A-Mrazek Moving Systems, the Arizona Cardinals, Custom Cuts, Dream Factory, FedEx Office, For Those Without a

Voice, Give Kids the World, Horizon Moving Systems, Hostway, Insight, Joyce Meyer Ministries, Logo Joe's, Make-A-Wish Foundation, Marketplace One, Missouri and Illinois credit unions, Missouri and Illinois police stations, NFL Charities, Nike, Operation Food Search, Packages From Home, Priority Sports & Entertainment, ProSource, Roth Capital Partners, U-Haul, University of Phoenix, Wal-Mart, and Walt Disney World Resorts. (We apologize if anyone was inadvertently omitted.)

Last but not least, we want to thank Marci Pritts and Jennifer Zink, who are our hands behind the scenes. We are thrilled to work beside them while calling them friends. We are blessed to have so many people in our lives that share a vision to change this world for the better. You make it easier to do that when you come to work, loving what you do. We love you and thank you.

For more information,
visit the First Things First Foundation Web site at
www.kurtwarner.org.

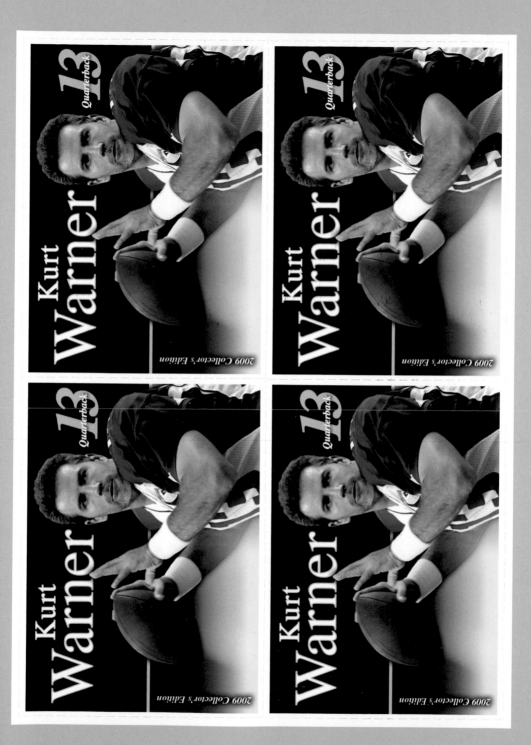

trading cards

Do you ever think about your legacy?

How will others remember you? This was the prevailing question for me at Super Bowl XLIII. People expected talk about NFL records, MVPs, and Super Bowls, but those things have little significance in how I want to be remembered. The greatest person I know set an example of excellence and used it to inspire others to do the same. His name is Jesus. Although I will never meet his standard, my desire is to create a similar legacy. The key to achieving this goal is in knowing and following Jesus Christ. If your desire is to build an eternal legacy, I encourage you to find Jesus today.

Say This Simple Prayer:

Lord Jesus, you know everything about me. Please forgive me for all the wrong things I've ever said or done. I know that you died for my sins and rose from the dead. Please come into my life and be my Lord. Help me to follow you always. Amen.

Read the Bible · Attend Church
Pray to God · Tell Others about Jesus
WWW.KURTWARNER.ORG / WWW.FUTUREANDHOPE.ORG
THIS CARD IS NOT AFFILIATED WITH OR ENDORSED BY THE ARIZONA CARDINALS,
THE NFL, OR NFL PROPERTIES ©2009 KW

Kurt Warner
Quarterback

Born 6 · 22 · 71
Burlington, IA
Ht 6'2" | Wt 220
Born Again 6 · 20 · 96

Do you ever think about your legacy?

How will others remember you? This was the prevailing question for me at Super Bowl XLIII. People expected talk about NFL records, MVPs, and Super Bowls, but those things have little significance in how I want to be remembered. The greatest person I know set an example of excellence and used it to inspire others to do the same. His name is Jesus. Although I will never meet his standard, my desire is to create a similar legacy. The key to achieving this goal is in knowing and following Jesus Christ. If your desire is to build an eternal legacy, I encourage you to find Jesus today.

Say This Simple Prayer:

Lord Jesus, you know everything about me. Please forgive me for all the wrong things I've ever said or done. I know that you died for my sins and rose from the dead. Please come into my life and be my Lord. Help me to follow you always. Amen.

Read the Bible · Attend Church
Pray to God · Tell Others about Jesus
WWW.KURTWARNER.ORG / WWW.FUTUREANDHOPE.ORG
THIS CARD IS NOT AFFILIATED WITH OR ENDORSED BY THE ARIZONA CARDINALS,
THE NFL, OR NFL PROPERTIES ©2009 KW

Kurt Warner
Quarterback

Born 6 · 22 · 71
Burlington, IA
Ht 6'2" | Wt 220
Born Again 6 · 20 · 96

Do you ever think about your legacy?

How will others remember you? This was the prevailing question for me at Super Bowl XLIII. People expected talk about NFL records, MVPs, and Super Bowls, but those things have little significance in how I want to be remembered. The greatest person I know set an example of excellence and used it to inspire others to do the same. His name is Jesus. Although I will never meet his standard, my desire is to create a similar legacy. The key to achieving this goal is in knowing and following Jesus Christ. If your desire is to build an eternal legacy, I encourage you to find Jesus today.

Say This Simple Prayer:

Lord Jesus, you know everything about me. Please forgive me for all the wrong things I've ever said or done. I know that you died for my sins and rose from the dead. Please come into my life and be my Lord. Help me to follow you always. Amen.

Read the Bible · Attend Church
Pray to God · Tell Others about Jesus
WWW.KURTWARNER.ORG / WWW.FUTUREANDHOPE.ORG
THIS CARD IS NOT AFFILIATED WITH OR ENDORSED BY THE ARIZONA CARDINALS,
THE NFL, OR NFL PROPERTIES ©2009 KW

Kurt Warner
Quarterback

Born 6 · 22 · 71
Burlington, IA
Ht 6'2" | Wt 220
Born Again 6 · 20 · 96

Do you ever think about your legacy?

How will others remember you? This was the prevailing question for me at Super Bowl XLIII. People expected talk about NFL records, MVPs, and Super Bowls, but those things have little significance in how I want to be remembered. The greatest person I know set an example of excellence and used it to inspire others to do the same. His name is Jesus. Although I will never meet his standard, my desire is to create a similar legacy. The key to achieving this goal is in knowing and following Jesus Christ. If your desire is to build an eternal legacy, I encourage you to find Jesus today.

Say This Simple Prayer:

Lord Jesus, you know everything about me. Please forgive me for all the wrong things I've ever said or done. I know that you died for my sins and rose from the dead. Please come into my life and be my Lord. Help me to follow you always. Amen.

Read the Bible · Attend Church
Pray to God · Tell Others about Jesus
WWW.KURTWARNER.ORG / WWW.FUTUREANDHOPE.ORG
THIS CARD IS NOT AFFILIATED WITH OR ENDORSED BY THE ARIZONA CARDINALS,
THE NFL, OR NFL PROPERTIES ©2009 KW

Kurt Warner
Quarterback

Born 6 · 22 · 71
Burlington, IA
Ht 6'2" | Wt 220
Born Again 6 · 20 · 96